T0135869

Technische Universität Braunschweig
Carl-Friedrich-Gauß-Fakultät
Institut für Betriebssysteme und Rechnerverbund

Multidimensional Transcoding for Adaptive Video Streaming

Von der Carl-Friedrich-Gauß-Fakultät

Technische Universität Carolo-Wilhelmina zu Braunschweig

zur Erlangung des Grades

Doktor-Ingenieur (Dr.-Ing.)

genehmigte

Dissertation

von Jens Brandt
geboren am 23.04.1975
in Gifhorn

Eingereicht am: 16.10.2009
Mündliche Prüfung am: 07.12.2009
Referent: Prof. Dr.-Ing. L. Wolf
Korreferent: Prof. Dr. P. Halvorsen

Bibliografische Information der Deutschen Nationalbibliothek

Die Deutsche Nationalbibliothek verzeichnet diese Publikation in der
Deutschen Nationalbibliografie; detaillierte bibliografische Daten sind
im Internet über http://dnb.d-nb.de abrufbar.

ISBN 978-3-8325-2390-9

Logos Verlag Berlin GmbH
Comeniushof, Gubener Str. 47,
10243 Berlin
Tel.: +49 (0)30 42 85 10 90
Fax: +49 (0)30 42 85 10 92
INTERNET: http://www.logos-verlag.de

Kurzfassung

Das Interesse an der Nutzung digitaler Videos unterliegt einem stetigen Wachstum. Schnellere Internetverbindungen und leistungsfähigere Geräte verhelfen der Videoübertragung über das Internet zu einer großen Popularität. Die Übertragung digitaler Videos deren und Wiedergabe auf mobilen Endgeräten mit einer drahtlosen Internetverbindung stößt jedoch weiterhin sehr schnell an seine Grenzen. Aufgrund stark beschränkter Ressourcen mobiler Geräte sowie den Eigenschaften drahtloser Netzwerkverbindungen ist eine fehlerfreie Übertragung und Darstellung qualitativ hochwertiger Videos über das Internet mit mobilen Geräten kaum möglich. Die Anzeige eines hochauflösenden Videos mit 1920×1080 Bildpunkten auf einem Gerät mit einer maximalen Auflösung von 320×240 Pixeln ist beispielsweise nicht ohne großen Berechnungsaufwand auf dem mobilen Gerät möglich. Die Übertragung des Videos belastet darüber hinaus den drahtlosen Kanal derart, dass Datenübertragungen anderer Geräte oder die Videoübertragung selbst erheblich gestört werden können. Eine Lösung dieses Problems besteht in der Anpassung der Videoströme an die jeweiligen Eigenschaften mobiler Geräte bereits während der Übertragung.

Im Rahmen dieser Arbeit wurden Protokolle und Mechanismen untersucht, die eine dynamische Anpassung von Videoströmen an die individuellen Eigenschaften mobiler Geräte ermöglichen. Dabei wurde ein Gateway System entwickelt, das die Anpassung von Videoströmen bereits während der Übertragung erlaubt. Für den Benutzer eines mobilen Gerätes arbeitet dieses System vollkommen transparent, da ein geeignetes Gateway automatisch aufgefunden und genutzt werden kann. Für die eigentliche Anpassung der Videoströme werden so genannte Transcodingtechniken eingesetzt, die eine komplette Dekodierung der Videoströme vermeiden.

Die ausschließliche Anpassung der räumlichen Auflösung eines Videos ist allerdings selten ausreichend, um den Gegebenheiten des empfangenden Gerätes gerecht zu werden. Stattdessen müssen häufig ebenfalls die zeitliche Auflösung sowie die Detailtiefe eines Videos angepasst werden. Existierende Ansätze beschränken sich jedoch auf die Anpassung einzelner und separat betrachteter Aspekte von Videoströmen. Im Rahmen dieser Arbeit wurde zunächst der Einfluss einer Anpassung verschiedener Dimensionen auf die Qualität des erzeugten Videostroms untersucht. Basierend auf den Ergebnissen konnte eine Empfehlung für eine mehrdimensionale Anpassung von Videoströmen gegeben werden. Für eine derartigen Anpassung wurde ein spezielles Transcodingverfahren entwickelt, das existierende eindimensionale Verfahren zu einem mehrdimensionalen Transcoder kombiniert. Mit dem Einsatz dieses Transcodingverfahrens auf dem entwickelten Gateway ist es möglich, verschiedenen mobilen Geräten eine individuelle und dynamische Anpassung von Videoströmen an deren spezifische Gegebenheiten anzubieten.

Abstract

The prominence of digital video on the Internet is rising constantly. Faster Internet connections and more powerful devices make video streaming over the Internet more and more popular. With mobile devices, however, the usability of digital videos that are streamed over a wireless network connection is still limited by the available resources. Mobile devices are often not capable of receiving and decoding high quality video streams from the Internet because of their limited resources as well as due to the limitations of a wireless network connection. The presentation, for instance, of a video stream with 1920×1080 pixels on a screen with a resolution of only 320×240 pixels is not possible without a high amount of processing power at the receiving device. The transmission of such a high quality video stream over a wireless link may additionally consume a large part of the available network capacity, which then may interfere active network connections of other devices. A limited network capacity may additionally prevent the device from decoding and displaying the video stream at all. One solution of these problems is to perform an adaptation of the video stream to the requirements of mobile devices during the transmission of the stream to the client.

In this work we investigated different protocols and mechanisms that allow for dynamic adaptation of video streams to the requirements of mobile devices. Therefore, we developed a multimedia gateway system that provides video adaptation during the transmission of a stream to the client. This gateway system is working completely transparent for the user because the gateway can be discovered automatically by the client. For the process of video adaptation itself we concentrate on compressed domain video transcoding mechanisms that avoid a time-consuming complete decoding and encoding of the video stream.

An adaptation of solely the spatial resolution of the stream is typically not sufficient to meet the requirements of the requesting device. On the contrary, the spatial and the detail resolution may also need to be updated. Existing approaches, however, are mainly restricted to the adaptation of only one of these aspects. In this work we investigated the impact of different adaptation dimensions on the visual quality of the adapted stream. Based on these results, we were able to give a clear recommendation for a multidimensional adaptation of video streams. To be able to perform such an adaptation of video streams, we developed a novel transcoding architecture that facilitates a smart combination of existing one-dimensional transcoding mechanisms. By the use of this video transcoding approach at the proposed gateway system, individual and dynamic video adaptation services can be provided to mobile devices.

Acknowledgments

The way towards a doctoral thesis often is a stony path which sometimes opens out into a wide field and one has to keep track of the orientation towards one's goal. Now that I am at the end of this track, I would like to take the opportunity to thank all those people that helped and accompanied me during this long way until today. Without their help and support I would have never been able to accomplish this work.

First and foremost I would like to thank my adviser Prof. Dr.-Ing. Lars Wolf for his support and guidance during my research work. He gave me the opportunity to work at the Institut für Betriebssysteme und Rechnerverbund (IBR) and provided an excellent working environment with a great amount of personal freedom. I appreciate that he has always been willing to listen to my questions and concerns. His constructive comments always helped me to improve my work. Secondly, I would like to thank Prof. Dr. Pål Halvorsen for his great support during the last phase of my work. His valuable and extensive feedback helped me a lot to improve the presentation of my work.

The nice and open working environment at the IBR was very inspiring for me and I learned a lot during my time at the IBR. Therefore, I would also like to thank all my current and former colleagues for their openness and friendship. Especially, I would like to thank Oliver Wellnitz and Sven Lahde for all the fruitful and valuable discussions that were very inspiring and helpful during my research work.

Finally, I would like to thank those people that supported and encouraged me with their love and their familiar friendship at all times on my way towards this thesis: Birgit Ziegenmeyer, Kai Brandt, Ute and Günter Kalmbach, Suse Bähre and Anja Sand.

Jens Brandt, October 2009

Contents

List of Figures

List of Tables

Chapter 1

Introduction

Video streaming plays a decisive role on the Internet today and has attracted large interest in commercial as well as in research areas. The evolution of digital video coding and broadband Internet access enable a large number of users to access high quality video streams today. Many devices are used by various groups of customers in numerous business-related or private situations. User-scenarios that need to be accounted for have been changing dynamically over the last years. Today they range from teenagers who are interested in watching some online video clips on their mobile phones to business people watching the latest video news via a wireless network connection on their notebooks. Digital video streaming over any kind of network, however, is still characterized by its particularly high resource requirements, concerning both the transmission and the decoding of video streams. Especially mobile devices often cannot comply with such resource demands because their ability of video streaming is restricted by the available resources on the devices. When looking at a typical current mobile device such as a PDA, a smartphone or a pocket multimedia player we can find a processor speed of about 400 – 800 MHz and a memory size up to several hundred MB. The screen resolution varies from very small displays of mobiles phones with less than 128×160 pixels to PDAs with VGA resolution (640×480) displays or even higher.

Digital video streams, on the other hand, typically have nearly the opposite characteristics because of their higher resource demands. High quality video streams have high data rates and therefore, compression methods are needed to reduce the amount of video data. Often a lossy compression method is chosen which in turn leads to higher processing power demands to decode and display the video. The primary problem with mobile devices and their limited resources is that they are typically incapable of decoding and displaying high quality video streams from the Internet without any support from special video decoding hardware. Although the resources of such devices are constantly increasing, this problem will remain in the near future, since quality demands are rising as well. Further problems may occur in the case of video streaming with mobile devices over wireless networks. Due to the wireless transmission, the usable data rates may be low and data may get lost during the transmission. In addition to these hardware related issues, mobile devices typically also support only a limited set of video encoding formats and encoding parameters. This may prevent a device from decoding a certain stream which limits the user to only consume those streams that are encoded in the "right" format.

One key technology needed for video streaming with mobile devices is video adaptation. By the use of video adaptation the gap between the characteristics of digital video on the one hand and mobile devices on the other hand can be closed, as the video streams can be individually adapted to the capabilities of the requesting device.

1.1 Video Adaptation

The market of mobile devices is constantly growing The manufacturers launch new devices at frequent intervals. To comply with different user demands the diversity of these devices is increasing as well. In the context of digital video streaming, this heterogeneity of mobile devices as well as rising video quality demands result in the problem that not all of these devices can process and display all available video streams. If, for instance, the spatial resolution of a video stream is higher than the display resolution of a device, it needs to downscale each video frame to be able to display it on its screen. This scaling process consumes additional processing power that is not always available on mobile devices. Another example is that a device does not support the encoding format of the video stream which prevents the device from decoding the stream at all. In both examples, the device of a user who would like to view a certain video stream cannot process and display the video stream per se due to some limitations of the device. One solution would be to provide each available video stream in different versions, at different resolutions, in different encoding formats, at different quality levels, or with even more different encoding parameters. This could obviously result in a high number of different versions to support the great heterogeneity of video capable devices. Additionally, the user of the device would need to know about his or her device capabilities in order to chose the "right" version of the video stream he or she is interested in.

A more flexible solution could be the use of individual and fine-grained adaptation of the video stream to the capabilities of the requesting device. Figure 1.1 shows some examples of different adaptation methods. The temporal adaptation reduces the number of frames in the stream. This, for instance, would be suitable for a device that can only process low frame rates. The detail adaptation reduces the details visible in the frames which also reduces the bit rate of the stream. This adaptation approach might be useful for slow network connections. A third example refers to spatial adaptation. By reducing the spatial resolution of each video frame a given stream could be tailored to the probably small screen resolution of the requesting device.

Almost all video streams that can be found on the Internet today are provided in a compressed format such as MPEG-4 video [1] in order to save storage and network capacities. Because of this compressed nature of digital video streams, the single video frames and their pixels are not directly accessible in the stream and therefore, the whole video stream cannot be modified directly. Before the pixels of the video frames can be manipulated, the frames need to be decompressed first. After the necessary

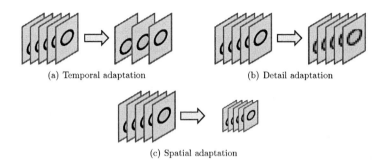

(a) Temporal adaptation   (b) Detail adaptation

(c) Spatial adaptation

Figure 1.1: Adaptation of different video dimensions

adaptation of the stream to the requirements of the client, the video frames need to be compressed again in order to be transmitted over the network. Video compression is a time consuming task as every single frame of the stream needs to be compressed. Thus, the procedure of decompressing and then compressing a video stream is obviously even more costly in terms of processing time. Moreover, digital video compression typically utilizes temporal redundancies contained between successive frames to reduce the number of bits needed to encode each frame. This is achieved by introducing some dependencies between successive frames which typically prevent a discarding of complete frames from the stream.

However, it is also possible to adapt a video stream without completely decoding it by using so-called compressed domain transcoding techniques. With compressed domain transcoding the processing time needed for video adaptation can be reduced significantly as some of the time consuming decoding and encoding steps are avoided. Working in the compressed domain, however, is typically more complex. Firstly, the pixel values are not directly available in the compressed stream. Secondly, most operations on a compressed video stream introduce a transcoding error that needs to be reduced by refining the dependencies between successive frames. This higher complexity typically also limits the flexibility of operations that can be performed on the video frames. Thus, video adaptation in the compressed domain is only possible at the expense of lower flexibility and higher complexity compared to an adaptation of uncompressed video. In comparison to the complete adaptation process that consists of decompression, adaptation, and then compression again, compressed domain transcoding can save those compression and decompression steps that consume a high amount of processing power. The processing power needed to adapt a stream, nevertheless, is still quite high. Therefore, the adaptation should not be performed on the presenting device itself as this usually has only limited resources. Instead, the video stream should be adapted before the stream is transmitted to the client, which also reduces the amount of data transmitted over the wireless link to the client.

Compared to other data types that are transferred over the Internet such as text and images or audio information, video streams are quite complex in nature. Many different aspects define or influence the characteristics of digital video streams. In the context of video adaptation, all of these aspects need to be considered in order to get reasonable results. Thus, to achieve a fine-grained video adaptation we have to take into account that there are several different encoding parameters that affect the quality as well as the resource requirements of a video stream. As mentioned before, adaptation of the spatial resolution is used to adjust the resolution of a video stream to the display resolution of a requesting device. This process also reduces the memory and processor requirements on the device. Adaptation of the temporal resolution as well as adaptation of the detail resolution can be used for further bit rate reduction. In addition to the adaptation of these three resolutions, video streams can also be adapted by semantic modifications, such as cropping the video to a central region of interest or reducing the video to a few key sequences. However, none of these one-dimensional approaches seems to be sufficient to meet all of the requirements defined by the capabilities of a client involved in any specific digital video streaming scenario. In most cases an adaptation in more than one dimension is needed, in order to tailor the video to the requirements of the requesting device as well as to the user's preferences.

1.2 Scenario and Approach

The target scenario of this work is a typical video streaming scenario with mobile clients as illustrated in figure 1.2. Mobile clients can connect to the Internet by using a wireless network connection of a network provider. The network that contains the access points is called the access network. This network usually contains infrastructure components that are needed to operate the access network and to provide a connection to the Internet for mobile clients. Examples of such access networks are the network of a provider that operates wireless LAN hot-spots [2] in a city or cellular radio networks such as GSM and UMTS [3].

Apart from the infrastructure components that are needed to operate the network, the provider may also include some content servers and gateways in the access network. Gateways may provide services that enhance the usability of the network or services that reduce network usage. In case of multimedia streaming, a caching proxy, for instance, could reduce the traffic between the access network and the Internet. This is achieved by storing popular media streams on the proxy so that future client requests can be served directly by the proxy without transmitting the video stream from the server another time. Multimedia gateways that provide video adaptation services to mobile clients are another example of such components that may enhance the usability of the access network.

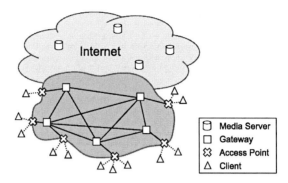

Figure 1.2: Target scenario

The goal of this work is to provide individual video adaptation services to mobile clients in such video streaming scenarios as described above. Therefore, we derived the following requirements which have to be considered in a future video adaption system:

(1) Video streams can be tailored to the requirements of the receiving client which are defined by the capabilities of the mobile device as well as the user's preferences;

(2) Different adaptation techniques should be available at the adaptation system to satisfy the demands of different users and devices;

(3) The adaptation system should be transparent from the user's perspective;

(4) The mobility of the users should be supported by the adaptation system;

(5) The system should be interoperable with existing streaming solutions.

In this thesis we present a novel transcoding architecture for multidimensional video adaptation that can be used to achieve the requirements (1) and (2). To make this adaptation mechanism available to mobile clients, we also present a multimedia gateway architecture that meets the other aforementioned requirements. To meet the requirement (3) we use several gateways which can be located automatically by a proposed gateway discovery mechanism. Additionally, the requirements of the client can be exchanged during session setup. As cooperation between our gateways is also supported, we can also achieve criterion (4) because this cooperation facilitates a session hand-off. The cooperation additionally enables a distributed caching mechanism that reduces the network load between the access network and the media servers. To support requirement (5) we use widely used standard streaming mechanisms and protocols as far as possible.

1.3 Contributions

The main contribution of this thesis is a novel approach for multidimensional video transcoding that enables a comprehensive video adaptation to the requirements of a requesting client. Further contributions of this thesis cover different aspects of the multimedia gateway architecture that makes these video adaptation mechanisms available to mobile devices. In particular, the contributions of this thesis are:

- **Multimedia Gateway Architecture:** In this work we present a novel multimedia gateway architecture that provides multimedia adaptation services to mobile clients. The main goals of this architecture are to be as flexible as possible and to be easy to use for mobile clients, as we presented in [4, 5, 6]. Therefore, our architecture and implementation include the following features:

  - *flexible stream reflection* to save network capacity,
  - *extendable data path* to use different adaptation libraries,
  - *capability exchange* to get information about the capabilities of a client,
  - *gateway discovery* to let clients automatically locate a gateway,
  - *cooperative caching* to reduce network load at media servers.

- **Multidimensional Video Adaptation:** For providing optimal video adaptation services to mobile clients, we analyze the quality that can be achieved by video adaptation in the three most important adaptation dimensions, which are the temporal, the spatial, and the detail dimension. Based on this analysis we give a clear recommendation how digital video streams should be adapted for mobile devices in these dimensions.

- **Multidimensional Video Transcoding:** We propose a novel processing architecture for video adaptation that facilitates a combination of several one-dimensional transcoding mechanisms into a transcoder chain that provides multidimensional video adaptation. The usability of this processing architecture will be shown by presenting a multidimensional MPEG-4 transcoder implementation. We presented this multidimensional video transcoding approach in [7, 8].

- **Video Content Analysis:** For content analysis of the processed video streams we define several measures that allow content analysis in the compressed domain. The usability of these measures will be shown with a fast frame-based scene change detection algorithm that is completely working with compressed domain information, as we presented in [9].

1.4 Scope

The scope of our work is video streaming and video adaptation for mobile devices. As introduced above, we discuss numerous core issues related to the adaptation and transcoding of digital video streams as well as the analysis of video content within video sequences. There are further aspects that we do not concentrate on in our work. Although being important issues, they can be treated separately and do not influence our approaches. Therefore, the following aspects are out of scope of this thesis.

- **Audio Adaptation:** Digital video streams typically also contain audio information that could be adapted to the capabilities of the requesting client as well. Compared to the visual information the fraction of the audio information is quite low and therefore also the gain that can be achieved with audio adaptation. Additionally, the nature of audio streams is much less complex compared to video streams. There are, for instance, no temporal dependencies within the streams and different audio channels can be separated easily.

- **Link Capacity Measurement:** In the context of digital video streaming, video adaptation is needed not only to meet the requirements of the requesting device, but also to fit to the capacity of the possibly wireless channel to the client. With our multidimensional transcoding architecture this can be achieved as well. However, measuring and estimating the current channel capacity and other conditions need to be done with additional components that are not part of our work, but could be integrated into our proposed system.

1.5 Outline

This thesis presents our contributions towards multidimensional video adaptation as well as our multidimensional video transcoding approach for individual video adaptation. It further describes our multimedia gateway architecture to provide video adaptation services to mobile clients and is organized as follows:

- **Chapter 2** provides detailed information about the background of this work in general as well as about different base technologies that we use in this work. This chapter includes an overview of widely used video encoding standards as well as details about the core mechanisms that are used in these standards. For video transmission we concentrate on standard IETF protocols that are shortly introduced as well. Afterwards we concentrate on video adaptation in general and on compressed domain video transcoding in particular. Thereby, we present several existing approaches from the literature that we refer to or use later on in this work.

- **Chapter 3** gives an overview of our multimedia gateway architecture that we developed in order to provide adaptation services to mobile clients. We present the core design issues of the proposed architecture, which mainly result from the used protocols as well as from the ability of this gateway to act as a flexible reflector. Clients that would like to use the gateway need to be able to address the gateway which is achieved by the integration of a gateway discovery mechanisms. Before the gateway may adapt any stream to the requirements of the requesting device, it needs to get information about the capability of the device which can be achieved by a capability exchange mechanism. To reduce the network load between the gateway and the media servers we also included caching capabilities that can be used cooperatively by several neighboring gateways. All these features are covered in this chapter.

- **Chapter 4** presents the main focus of this work, i.e., the multidimensional video transcoding. In the first part, we analyze video adaptation for mobile devices in general and identify three main adaptation dimensions that need to be tailored in order to support a great range of different devices. Afterwards, we inspect these adaptation dimensions more closely and present measurement results about the quality that can be achieved by adaptation of these dimensions individually. Based on these results, we propose a multidimensional transcoding approach in section 4.2 that uses a modular and flexible processing architecture. The prototype implementation of a multidimensional MPEG-4 transcoder that uses this architecture is presented afterwards. The evaluation results of the quality that is produced by our implementation as well as its runtime are presented at the end of this part. The third part of chapter 4 deals with compressed domain content analysis that can be used during the transcoding process. In order to achieve this, we define different measures and histograms that can be computed very fast without decoding the video frames. An example of how these measures can be used is given by a fast and frame-based scene change detection algorithm.

- **Chapter 5** finally concludes this thesis with a summary of what we presented in this work and some directions of further research in the context of video adaptation for mobile devices.

Chapter 2

Background and Base Technologies

The prominence of digital video on the Internet is rising constantly. Advances in video coding as well as an increasing available bandwidth make video streaming across a wide range of different networks possible. However, due to its high data rates as well as its time-critical nature, special encoding mechanisms and protocols are needed for high-quality video streaming. In this chapter we give an overview about the mechanisms and approaches in the context of digital video streaming which we concentrate on in this work. We start with a brief introduction to digital video coding in section 2.1, where we introduce fundamental mechanisms which are used by popular video coding standards. Afterwards, we shortly describe some key protocols which are widely used for video streaming on the Internet in section 2.2. In section 2.3 we discuss different aspects of video adaptation in general, including a subsection about scalable video coding. Afterwards, we give detailed information about video transcoding for single layer video adaptation in section 2.4. The main focus of that section is compressed domain transcoding. Here we present different mechanisms that are important base technologies for our video adaptation approach which is described later in this work, in chapter 4. Section 2.5 gives an overview of existing video adaptation systems, proposed in the literature that also use similar transcoding techniques. One important aspect in the context of digital video in general as well as in the context of video adaptation is the measurement of video quality. In section 2.6 we present a well-known video quality metric which we use in our work to evaluate the video quality produced by our approach.

2.1 Video Coding

Digital video can hardly ever be transmitted on the Internet without any compression. Due to the great amount of data that is involved in producing high quality video streams, digital video needs to be compressed in nearly all streaming-related situations. Therefore, the International Telecommunication Union (ITU) as well as the International Organization for Standardization (ISO) have defined several different standards for digital video coding. The ITU's Telecommunication Standardization Sector (ITU-T) started in 1990 with the first practical video compression standard H.261 [10], which was designed mainly to support video conferencing with low bit rates. With MPEG-1

[11], ISO defined its first video coding standard in 1993 which should achieve better quality at bit rates of about 1.5 Mbit/s. Based on both standards, ITU and ISO then jointly developed the MPEG-2 [12] standard which is based on both previous standards and focuses on video coding for digital television. A first version of this standard was published in 1994. Today, MPEG-2 video is widely used for Digital Versatile Discs (DVD) and Digital Video Broadcasting (DVB) in several countries. The next standard for digital video coding, which was published by ITU in 1995, was H.263 [13]. The visual quality achieved by H.263 was much better than for all previous encoding standards. At the same time ISO started working on the MPEG-4 [1] video coding standard, which was firstly published in 1999 as MPEG-4 part 2. MPEG-4 video is very similar to H.263, but also includes several novel video coding concepts like object based coding, shape coding, face and body animation, as well as 3D graphics.

However, most of these video coding concepts introduced with MPEG-4 video are still not widely used and ISO has concentrated more on regular video coding in recent year. This again resulted in a joint development. ITU and ISO started developing the MPEG-4 Advanced Video Coding (AVC) [14] standard, which is also known as MPEG-4 part 10 or H.264. AVC is mainly based on MPEG-4 part 2, but uses more enhanced features, such as enhanced prediction modes and entropy coding. The first version of AVC was published in 2003.

In our work we concentrate on video, which is encoded following MPEG-4 part 2. Therefore, we are using the term *MPEG-4 video* as a synonym for natural video encoded according to the MPEG-4 part 2 standard [1] for the rest of this document. Our approach, however, is not limited to MPEG-4 video. It can be easily extended to support AVC, as AVC is based on MPEG-4 video and uses very similar features.

The overall aim of video coding is to reduce the data rate of digital video stream while at the same time keeping an acceptable quality level. In general, the different video coding standards, defined either by ITU or ISO, use similar mechanisms to achieve this aim of reducing the data rate of digital video. Spatial redundancies within single frames of a digital video sequence are exploited by *intra frame coding*. Temporal redundancies of successive frames are typically used to reduce the data rate by *inter frame coding*. Additionally, lossless *entropy encoding* as well as lossy quantization are used as two mechanisms to reduce the number of non-zero values. All aforementioned video coding standards define block-based video coding mechanisms that use the discrete cosine transform (DCT) [15] to reduce spatial redundancies and motion compensation (MC) mechanisms to remove temporal redundancies. In this section we introduce some of these fundamental concepts and mechanisms which are used by the major standards for video coding.

2.1.1 Intra Frame Coding

Digital video consists of video frames which are very similar to digital still images. Each single frame contains redundant information, such as neighboring pixels with the same color or even bigger regions with the same texture. These spatial redundancies can be exploited for reducing the amount of data needed to store each single frame. This mechanism for encoding each single frame is called *intra frame coding*. The intra frame coding is similar to still image encoding. Each video frame is divided into blocks of 8×8 pixels which are transformed into the frequency domain by using the DCT that is defined as follows:

$$F_{u,v} = \frac{C(u)C(v)}{4} \sum_{i=0}^{7} \sum_{j=0}^{7} f_{i,j} cos \left(\frac{(2i+1)u\pi}{16} \right) cos \left(\frac{(2j+1)v\pi}{16} \right) \qquad (2.1)$$

with $f_{i,j}$ being the value of the pixel at position (i,j) of the current pixels block, $F_{u,v}$ being the DCT value at position (u,v) of the resulting DCT block, and $C(w)$ being a constant with

$$C(w) = \begin{cases} \frac{1}{\sqrt{2}} & \text{for } w = 0 \\ 1 & \text{otherwise.} \end{cases} \qquad (2.2)$$

The result from the DCT operation is a block of 8×8 DCT values. As every pixel value is involved in the computation of every single DCT value, these values carry information about the whole block. Due to spatial redundancies within the blocks, the number of zero values in the transformed blocks is much higher than in the pixel blocks, which allows more efficient encoding than before. Figure 2.1 shows an example of a grayscale 8×8 pixels block on the left with its corresponding pixel values in the middle and the DCT values on the right. The value of the lowest frequency, which is called the DC value, is always located in the upper left corner of the transformed block. The other values are called AC values. The low frequency values are most important, because they carry the most information of the block. The high frequency values are located in the lower right part of the transformed block and are less important. In the case of color video streams, the DCT is computed for each color component separately.

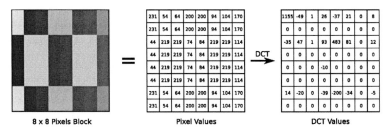

Figure 2.1: DCT example for one grayscale 8 × 8 pixels block

The inverse computation of the two-dimensional DCT is defined as follows:

$$f_{i,j} = \frac{1}{4} \sum_{u=0}^{7} \sum_{v=0}^{7} C(u)C(v)F_{u,v} cos\left(\frac{(2i+1)u\pi}{16}\right) cos\left(\frac{(2j+1)v\pi}{16}\right) \qquad (2.3)$$

with the pixel values $f_{i,j}$, the DCT values $F_{u,v}$, and the constant $C(w)$ as given before in equations 2.1 and 2.2.

Instead of calculating the DCT values of an 8×8 pixels block a by using equation 2.1, it is also possible to compute the DCT block A from block a as

$$A = DCT(a) = TaT^t, \qquad (2.4)$$

where T is the 8×8 DCT matrix with coefficients given by

$$T_{i,j} = \frac{1}{2}C(i)cos\left(\frac{(2j+1)i\pi}{16}\right) \qquad (2.5)$$

with the constant $C(w)$ as defined in equation 2.2. This alternative notation of the DCT gives an idea of the complexity of the DCT computation, as two matrix multiplications are needed per 8×8 pixels block. However, several fast algorithms that are using matrix decomposition methods were proposed, such as the approach proposed by Feig and Winograd in [16].

Quantization

The quantization process is a very important step in video encoding as it mainly controls the produced quality of intra-coded frames as well as the compression level of the video stream. Due to the nature of human perception, changes of the higher frequency values can hardly be noticed by the user. This situation can be exploited to further reduce the number of bits needed for the video stream: The DCT values can be quantized in a way that reduces the number of non-zero AC values. The simplest quantization can be achieved by dividing each DCT value by a constant value and rounding the result to the nearest integer value. Some video coding standards define a quantization process that uses a quantization matrix as well as a quantizer scale value. MPEG-4, for instance, defines two different quantization methods. The first quantization method computes the quantized DCT values $QF_{u,v}$ from the DCT values $F_{u,v}$ and the coefficients of the quantization matrix $W_{u,v}$ as follows:

$$QF_{u,v} = \frac{F_{u,v}\frac{16}{W_{u,v}} - k \cdot quantiser\_scale}{2 \cdot quantiser\_scale} \qquad (2.6)$$

where

$$k = \begin{cases} 0 & \text{for intra-coded blocks} \\ sign(QF_{u,v}) & \text{for inter-coded blocks.} \end{cases} \qquad (2.7)$$

All divisions in equation 2.6 are integer divisions with rounding to the nearest integer. The quantization process is controlled by the quantization matrix as well as the quantizer scale value. This value ranges from 1 to 31 and directly affects the bit rate of the stream. The higher the quantizer scale value, the more DCT values are discarded and the lower is the number of visible details in the frame. MPEG-4 defines two default quantization matrices as shown in figure 2.2, one for intra-coded blocks and one for inter-coded blocks. If these matrices are used for quantization, they do not need to be saved in the video stream as they are defined in the standard. It is also possible to define other quantization matrices for each encoded video that, however, need to be saved in the video stream so that the decoder can use the same matrices for decoding the stream.

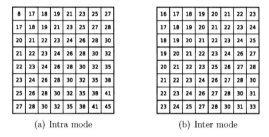

(a) Intra mode (b) Inter mode

Figure 2.2: Default quantization matrices for the MPEG quantization in MPEG-4

As the first quantization method is based on the method defined in the MPEG-2 video standard [12] it is often called MPEG quantization. The inverse MPEG quantization at the decoder to obtain the DCT values again is computed as follows:

$$F'_{u,v} = \begin{cases} 0 & \text{if } QF_{u,v} = 0 \\ \frac{(2 \cdot QF_{u,v} + k) \cdot W_{u,v} \cdot quantiser\_scale}{16} & \text{if } QF_{u,v} \neq 0 \end{cases} \qquad (2.8)$$

The second quantization method defined by MPEG-4 does not use quantization matrices. It is based on the method defined in H.263 [13] and is therefore also called H.263 quantization. The quantized DCT values $QF_{u,v}$ are computed from the DCT values $F_{u,v}$ as shown in the following equations:

$$|QF_{u,v}| = \begin{cases} |F_{u,v}| \ / \ 2 \cdot quantiser\_scale & \text{for intra-coded blocks} \\ (|F_{u,v}| - \frac{quantiser\_scale}{2}) \ / \ (2 \cdot quantiser\_scale) & \text{for inter-coded blocks} \end{cases} \qquad (2.9)$$

and

$$QF_{u,v} = Sign(F_{u,v}) \cdot |QF_{u,v}| \qquad (2.10)$$

The inverse H.263 quantization is computed by applying the following equation:

$$\left|F'_{u,v}\right| = \begin{cases} 0 & QF_{u,v} = 0 \\ (2\left|QF_{u,v}\right| + 1) \cdot quantiser\_scale & QF_{u,v} \neq 0, \text{odd } quantiser\_scale \\ (2\left|QF_{u,v}\right| + 1) \cdot quantiser\_scale - 1 & QF_{u,v} \neq 0, \text{even } quantiser\_scale \end{cases}$$

(2.11)

and

$$F'_{u,v} = Sign(QF_{u,v}) \cdot \left|F'_{u,v}\right|$$

(2.12)

Technically spoken, the quantization process controls the signal to noise ratio (SNR) of each video frame. The quantization process removes information from each frame, i.e., the signal and introduces some kind of distortion, i.e., some noise. The higher the quantizer scale value, the more values are discarded, and the more noise is produced. For a user who watches a digital video stream, the higher SNR results in fewer details visible in the stream. Detailed structures such as leafs of a tree or the texture of noisy water get lost due to a higher quantizer scale value. In our work we call this visibility of detailed structures the detail resolution of a video stream.

The limitation of the quantizer scale value to a rage from 1 to 31 also results in a lower bound for the bit rate of each video sequence. If the bit rate of the video stream needs to be below this bound, the frame rate or spatial resolution needs to be reduced.

2.1.2 Inter Frame Coding

Temporal redundancies within consecutive frames of a video provide the opportunity for further data reduction. Frames within video sequences are usually quite similar so that each frame carries much information which is already contained in the previous frame. Thus, by encoding only those parts of a frame which are different from the previous frame the number of bits can be lowered. In combination with motion estimation mechanisms, the amount of data for encoding those differences can be reduced even further.

Four neighboring 8×8 pixels blocks form a so-called macro block (MB), which is the basis of the motion estimation. Motion information is stored in the form of motion vectors (MV) which point to a similar region in a reference frame for each MB. Therefore, the MV contains the offset of the reference region for both the x- and the y-direction, in terms of pixels relative to the position of the current MB. How such a similar region can be found is not specified in any of the video coding standards. A simple encoder starts at the position of the current MB and searches within a limited search range of, for instance, ± 32 pixels to find the block with the smallest difference. The encoding error, which is introduced by using the referenced area of a previous frame instead of the original block, is encoded as the residual error block. In other words, only the differences between the current block and the reference block are encoded in the motion compensated frame. In case that the current MB does not differ from the MB in the previous frame, the motion vector is zero and the residual error blocks also contain zero values only. A MB with a zero length motion vector that contains no other values than zeros is also called a not coded or skipped MB as zero values does not need to be encoded. In all other cases the motion vector may point to an area where the number of non-zero values of the residual error block is minimized. To enlarge the number of possible reference blocks, most of the aforementioned video coding standards define the possibility to search for reference blocks not only in previous, but also in following frames. This minimizes the number of non-zero values, and in this case, up to one forward and one backward motion vector can be stored in the MB.

Finding a MB in a previous or possibly following frame is not always possible. In the case of a scene change, for instance, the frame differs typically completely from any previous frame. In such a situation, the values of the residual error block may need more bits to be encoded than the original values of the current MB. Thus, no suitable reference block could be found in any reference frame and it would be better to encode the original values of the current MB. Therefore, it is possible to encoded single MBs in intra-coded mode, i.e., by using the intra frame coding methods, although the rest of the frame is encoded with the inter frame coding method.

At decoding time, the motion compensation needs to be inverted to reconstruct the original video frames. For each motion compensated MB the original values can be recomputed by using the values of the block that is referenced by the MV and the residual error that is encoded for the current block.

2.1.3 Frame Types

In a video sequence at least one frame, i.e., the first frame, needs to be encoded completely so that it can be used as a reference frame for the motion compensation. This is achieved by the use of intra frame coding for the first frame. All following frames may be encoded using inter frame coding. However, for random access as well as for error recovery, an intra-coded frame should be inserted from time to time. Additionally, the motion estimation might fail for some MBs, so that no suitable reference block can be found. In that case, also inter-coded frames may contain some intra-coded blocks as described before. Mainly three different frames can be distinguished within a digital video sequence:

- I-frames are completely encoded frames without any dependencies to other frames. Thus, only intra frame coding mechanisms without motion estimation are used for frame encoding. I-frames are also called key frames.

- P-frames are inter encoded frames which use a previous P- or I-frame as reference. All contained motion vectors point into the same reference frame.

- B-frames are similar to P-frames but use two reference I- or P-frames, one previous and one following frame.

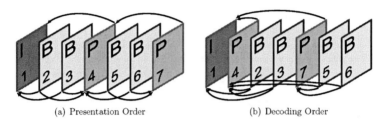

(a) Presentation Order   (b) Decoding Order

Figure 2.3: Frame types in different orders

Figure 2.3(a) illustrates these different frame types in a typical combination. The first frame of a sequence obviously needs to be an I-frame that contains all information about the frame. In this example the next two frames are B-frames that use the previous I-frame as well as the following P-frame as reference frames. The P-frames uses solely the previous I- or P-frame as the reference frame. The numbers in the figure illustrate the order in which the frames are presented. Because B-frames may additionally use forward motion vectors that point into future frames, it is necessary that those future frames are available in the decoder before the decoding process of the B-frame may start. Therefore, the decoding order of the frames may differ from their presentation order. That means that those frames which are referenced by B-frames need to be decoded before the referencing frame, as illustrated in figure 2.3(b). The P-frame with the number 4, for instance, needs to be decoded before the B-frames 2 and 3 can be decoded.

Compared to previous video coding standards, the MPEG-4 standard introduced several new features such as an inherent support for object based video coding. With the existence of video objects the concept of video frames that contain all information at a certain point of time in the stream is not sufficient any more. Instead the more flexible concept of video object planes (VOP) was introduced in the MPEG-4 video standard. A VOP is a representation of all video objects of the current video stream at a certain point in time. Similar to streams with video frames, an MPEG-4 video stream consists of several encoded VOPs. Accordingly to the aforementioned I-, P- and B-frames, the MPEG-4 standard defines I-, P- and B-VOPs. For some special situations, the MPEG-4 video standard also supports to encode a VOP as a so-called N-VOP. An N-VOP is a non-coded or skipped frame that is decoded like an inter-coded frame with a zero length motion vector and a residual error that contains only zero values. This special VOP can be used in video streams that contain several non-changing frames. An example of such a stream is a slide show that shows every slide a couple of seconds without any changes.

2.1.4 Entropy Coding

The data of each video frame which was produced by intra or inter frame coding mechanisms finally needs to be encoded as efficiently as possible. This is the task of the entropy coding. Before the DCT values of a block can be encoded they need to be serialized. Therefore, different scanning methods exist which define the order in which the values are read from a block and put into a sequence. The classic scanning method is called zig-zag scanning, which is also used in still image compression. The zig-zag scan starts with the most important value of a block, i.e., the DC value, and serializes the AC values in zig-zag order from the upper left to the lower right coordinate, as shown in figure 2.4(a). MPEG-4 video defines two alternative scanning methods: the alternate-horizontal scan as shown in figure 2.4(b) and the alternate-vertical scan method as shown in figure 2.4(c).

    (a) Zig-zag scan   (b) Alternate-horizontal scan   (c) Alternate-vertical scan

Figure 2.4: Different scan methods

All three scanning methods exploit the special structure of the DCT values and start with the DC value in the upper left corner of the block. This scanning typically results in long sequences of zeros which are removed by using some run-length encoding (RLE). The RLE compresses long sequences of the same value by storing its length and the value. Finally, the resulting values can be further compressed by using entropy encoding techniques, which usually result in variable-length codes (VLC). A popular VLC is the Huffman-Code [17] which is used in many video coding standards.

Figure 2.5 schematically shows a simplified video encoder for MPEG video. This encoder consists of a DCT component which transfers the pixel values into the frequency domain before the quantizer component Q computes the quantized DCT values. The VLC component afterwards processes the entropy coding before the encoded video bitstream is produced. For the inter frame coding the shown feedback loop is used. In this loop firstly the inverse quantization (Q^{-1}) as well as secondly the inverse DCT (DCT^{-1}) is computed. The decoded frame is then stored in the frame store FS. The motion estimation component ME uses the frame store as well as the incoming frame

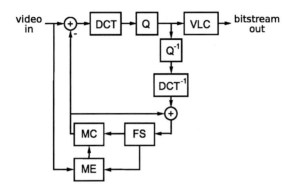

Figure 2.5: Simplified MPEG video encoder

to generate motion vectors for inter-coded frames. These motion vectors are used by the motion compensation module MC to compute the residual errors which are subtracted from the currently processed frame. The simplified decoder for MPEG video is shown in figure 2.6 and is much simpler than the video encoder. The decoder contains a component that computes the inverse entropy coding (VLC^{-1}). The DCT values are dequantized by the Q^{-1} component and transfered into the pixel domain by the DCT^{-1} component. The motion vectors are used by the motion compensation component MC that is used to reconstruct the video frame.

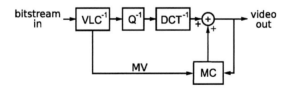

Figure 2.6: Simplified MPEG video decoder

2.2 Video Streaming

The transmission of continuous data flows is often called streaming. In contrast to traditional scenarios of downloading files from a server, a streaming scenario allows the client to start consuming the streaming data continuously right after receiving the first portions of the stream. In the case of digital video sequences a client may start decoding the stream right after it received the first parts of the first frame. Usually the client stores the streaming data only for the decoding process and discards each decoded frame as soon as all frames referencing to it are decoded. Only a small portion of the stream is stored in a buffer on the client side to reduce the effect of network jitter.

Video streaming on the Internet often uses protocols proposed by the Internet Engineering Task Force (IETF). For signaling purposes, the Real Time Streaming Protocol (RTSP) [18] which is a plain text request/response protocol at application layer is used. For data transport, the Real-time Control Protocol (RTP) [19] in conjunction with the User Datagram Protocol (UDP) [20] are used. These protocols are well-known and widely used on the Internet. We describe their main features in the next two sections.

2.2.1 RTSP

The Real Time Streaming Protocol (RTSP) [18] is used to control a streaming server from the client side. By using RTSP, a client may setup a streaming session with a streaming server. A streaming session is a logical construct which is used on the server side to maintain a certain state for the logical server-client connection. After session setup the client may use a set of methods to control the remote server in the same way as a media player running locally.

The most common RTSP messages are DESCRIBE, SETUP, PLAY, PAUSE, and TEARDOWN. Before session setup a client may use a DESCRIBE message to request detail information about a stream which is identified by an RTSP uniform resource identifier (URI). The response to such a request contains information about the stream, such as title and author, the encoding format or the duration of the stream. It is typically expressed by using the Session Description Protocol (SDP) [21]. With these details the client can establish the media session by sending a SETUP message to the server. The RTSP session is established after a positive response from the server. After session setup the client can start the streaming process by sending a PLAY message to the server which also contains the play time position of the stream. Figure 2.7(a) illustrates a typical RTSP communication between a client and a server: The client requests information about a certain stream, creates the session, and starts the streaming. After the positive response from the server to the PLAY message from the client, the server starts sending the data with RTP. The streaming session can be paused by sending a PAUSE message and terminated by sending a TEARDOWN message to the server. Seeking forward or backward in the stream can be achieved by sending a PAUSE message followed by a PLAY message with the new play time position to the server, as illustrated in figure 2.7(b).

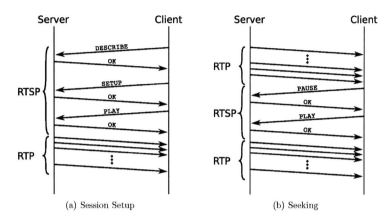

(a) Session Setup   (b) Seeking

Figure 2.7: RTSP communication

2.2.2 RTP

The available method of data transport for the media streams is also negotiated between a client and a streaming server during session setup. In combination with RTSP, the Real-time Control Protocol (RTP) [19] is typically used for application level framing and UDP [20] is used at the transport layer. For each media type an RTP payload type exists, which defines how the data of a stream needs to be partitioned to be transmitted in several datagrams. In case of an MPEG-4 video stream, for instance, the corresponding payload format defines that each RTP packet shall contain either one or several complete frames or a fragment of exactly one frame [22]. One complete frame and a fragment of the next frame, for instance, are not allowed within one single RTP packet.

Since RTP packets are usually transmitted by an unreliable transport protocol such as UDP, the receiving client needs to be able to detect any packet reordering or packet loss. RTP packets therefore contain a sequence number which is increased for each packet. For synchronization purposes, each packet additionally contains a time stamp. The frequency of this time stamp is defined for each payload type separately or negotiated at session setup between client and streaming server.

Due to the usage of an unreliable transport protocol, a second protocol that is called RTP Control Protocol (RTCP) is defined in [19]. RTCP can be used to inform both parties of a communication about transmitted or lost packets. Therefore, the server and the client periodically exchange sender and receiver reports to inform each other about the quality of the transmission. If the client, for instance, informs the server about lost packets, the server may react to this information by reducing its sending speed.

2.3 Video Adaptation

The characteristics of every digital video stream are defined by a combination of encoding parameters such as frame rate, spatial resolution or quality level at encoding time, which result in a certain bit rate of the stream. The best-effort nature of the Internet, however, cannot guarantee any required bandwidth for a certain connection. Every node involved in a video streaming session is bound to the encoding parameters of the video stream when handling it. Whenever the characteristics of a stream need to be changed, a complete re-encoding might be necessary and a number of problems might occur. The pixels of the video frames, for instance, cannot be modified directly because they are not accessible in the compressed stream. Another example are the dependencies between consecutive frames which were introduced by motion compensation mechanisms in the encoder. They result in fixed frame rates, and changes of the number of frames in the stream are not trivial.

However, efficient video adaptation is necessary to make high-quality video streams available to a great range of different devices. This section deals with these problems and describes different aspects of video adaptation, beginning with an introduction of adaptation dimensions in section 2.3.1. One possibility to support video adaptation is the use of scalable video encoding techniques, which are presented in 2.3.2. However, most video streams which can be found on the Internet today are encoded without scalability support as single layer video streams. Section 2.3.3 presents how these single layer video streams can still be adapted. The main focus in this work lies on compressed domain video transcoding, which is described afterwards in section 2.4.

2.3.1 Adaptation Dimensions

Digital video has a quite complex nature as several different aspects and parameters define the characteristics of a video stream. Two examples of such parameters are the frame rate of a video stream or the spatial resolution of each video frame within the stream. Moreover, also the video content itself can have a strong impact on the characteristics of the video stream. As we described before, the use of lossy compression techniques results in a compression ratio that depends on the amount of motion within a given video sequence. A higher amount of motion, for instance, results in a lower compression. When adapting a video stream to the requirements of a client, these characteristics of the video need to be changed in order to fit to the available resources on the network and at the requesting device. Thus, several different aspects of a video stream need to be considered and a number of methods to adapt these different aspects exist. In this work, we regard these aspects as different adaptation dimensions of the video stream:

- The *spatial dimension* is the number of pixels of a single frame in horizontal and vertical directions. Adaptation of this dimension can be used to adjust the video stream to the display resolution of the requesting device.

- The *temporal dimension* is the number of frames displayed in a certain period of time, usually given in frames per second (fps). By reducing the frame rate, the required bandwidth for transmission of a video stream is reduced as well.

- The *detail dimension* is the precision of details visible in each single frame. It is primarily controlled by the quantizer scale value used. By increasing this value, the detail resolution as well as the bit rate of the stream are reduced.

- The *syntactical dimension* defines the format of the bit stream. If a client, for instance, can decode MPEG-4 video only, a conversion of the bit stream from an MPEG-2 video to an MPEG-4 video could be used.

- The *structural dimension* contains everything related to the content of the stream. An adaptation of this dimension may be used to reduce the length of a video sequence by summarizing parts of the video. Another example of this kind of adaptation is watermarking or logo insertion, by which information is added to the video sequence.

Each adaptation dimension has a different focus. When a video stream needs to be adapted to the requirements of a requesting client, some dimensions will be more important than others. As we will see later on in this work, in section 4.1 about multidimensional video adaptation, the first three aforementioned dimensions play the most important role in the context of video adaptation for mobile clients. This list, however, is not intended to be exhaustive and several other adaptation dimensions may be possible. Another example in the structural dimension would be a cropping of video streams to a certain region of interest as described by Sinha et al. in [23].

2.3.2 Scalable Video Coding

MPEG-2 video [12] was the first video coding standard that addressed the problem of video scalability by introducing different video scalability modes for layered video encoding. With layered video coding the video stream is split up into a base layer and one or more enhancement layers. The base layer contains the video sequence in base quality and each enhancement layer contains further data which enhances the quality of the decoded sequence. A temporal scalability of the stream, for instance, can be achieved by using hierarchical prediction structures for the motion compensation. Then the base layer contains the video sequence with a low frame rate and the enhancement layers contain intermediate frames which use the frames from a lower layer as reference frames. Figure 2.8 illustrates such a video stream that contains one base layer with a low frame rate and one enhancement layer with intermediate frames. These additional frames are displayed between the frames of the base layer. Another possibility is spatial scalability, where the base layer contains each frame with a low spatial resolution and the enhancement layers contain the difference to the high resolution version of each frame. Another scalability objective may be the detail resolution of the video frames. This kind of scalability is called SNR scalability and may be achieved by using different quantizer scale values for different layers.

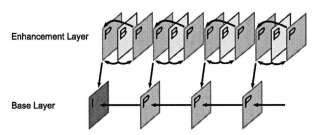

Figure 2.8: Temporal scalability

Based on the scalability modes defined in MPEG-2, MPEG-4 video also contains scalability support [1]. Similar to the MPEG-2 video standard, the MPEG-4 standard describes how temporal and spatial scalability can be achieved with MPEG-4 video. Additionally, MPEG-4 part 2 contains the Fine-Grained Scalable Video Coding (FGS) [1]. FGS is a special type of SNR scalability and defines one base layer which contains the video stream in low quality by using a high quantizer scale value. Further, FGS defines one enhancement layer which contains the reconstruction error introduced by the high quantizer scale value of the base layer. By using a bit plane representation of the DCT values in the enhancement layer, each single bit of the enhancement layer which is available at decoding time may enhance the quality of the decoded stream.

The most recent video coding standard which supports scalability is defined as an extension to MPEG-4 AVC [14] with the name Scalable Video Coding (SVC) [24]. Compared to previous approaches, SVC significantly improved the coding efficiency of layered video coding [25].

The main advantage of scalable or layered video coding is the possibility to handle each layer of the stream separately. Higher layers, for instance, can be removed without affecting the remaining layers of the stream. Thus, a video stream that was encoded with scalable video coding techniques, can be adapted to the requirements of a receiving device by discarding all those layers of the stream which exceed the capabilities of the requesting device or the capacity of the transmission channel.

In most cases where layered video is used, the adaptation of the stream according to the requirements of the client is accomplished either at the server or at the client. When streaming layered video over a network, an adaptation on intermediate nodes may also be promising. Rejaie and Kangasharju as well as Zhang et al. proposed two different proxy caches which are capable of discarding layers of video streams according to the available bandwidth in [26] and [27] respectively. A practical approach for discarding layers on an access point for home networks was presented by Kofler et al. in [28].

They proposed an RTSP/RTP proxy implemented on an access point that could be configured to discard all those packets that carry the same enhancement layer ID.

Due to its nature, layered video is well suited for multicast transmissions because each layer can be transmitted over a separate multicast tree. In this context, Liu et al. distinguishes two different approaches [29]: receiver driven multicast [30] and network driven multicast [31, 32]. In the former approach described by McCanne et al., each receiver tries to join as many multicast groups as its bandwidth allows. In the latter approach proposed by Vickers et al., all layers of a video stream are transmitted to the clients. If any router detects that there is no sufficient bandwidth available to transmit all layers, it will discard some layers of the stream, starting with the highest layer.

The intention of scalable video coding is to include scalability support directly into the video bit stream, which makes the adaptation of such streams quite simple. However, scalable video coding has some drawbacks that make additional adaptation mechanisms for single layer video streams necessary. First, the coding efficiency decreases with the degree of scalability as each additional layer introduces some overhead, which limits the reasonable number of layers [33]. Although the coding efficiency was improved with SVC, the overhead increases even further if several layers of a video stream are transmitted over the network as the header information needed for data transport and routing add even more overhead to each layer. A second restriction of layered video coding is the minimum bandwidth requirement of scalable video streams. As the base layer needs to be transmitted error-free to the clients, the bit rate of this layer defines the minimum bandwidth. If the rate at which a client may receive the stream is below the bit rate of the base layer, an adaptation of the base layer is needed. Layered video coding also makes higher demands on the requirements of the decoding device, as the decoding process is more complex compared to single layer video. Finally, today most video streams on the Internet as well as in the area of multimedia entertainment are encoded as single layer video streams without any scalability support, which calls for a different idea of video adaptation. In order to give an increasing number of different devices access to these widely existing streams, single layer video adaptation is needed.

2.3.3 Single Layer Video Adaptation

In the context of digital video, single layer video coding is widely used in current consumer electronics as well as on the Internet. Digital video broadcast (DVB) and popular Internet video platforms like, for instance, YouTube[1] provide solely single layer video streams. In contrast to layered video streams, single layer video streams cannot be adapted by simply dropping some portions of the streams. This is due to the dependencies between consecutive frames within a single layer video stream. Only those frames that are not used as reference frames can be dropped without influencing the decoding process. In case of MPEG-2 or MPEG-4 video this would only be true for B-frames

---

[1]http://www.youtube.com

which would not lead to a sufficient adaptation result for all adaptation dimensions. Thus, further adaptation mechanisms are needed that allow an adaptation of single layer video streams while maintaining or updating all existing dependencies.

The most obvious way to adapt digital video streams is to completely decode the stream, manipulate the pixels of each frame and encode the stream again. This approach was named a cascaded pixel domain transcoder (CPDT) by Youn et al. [34]. As illustrated in figure 2.9, the CPDT contains a complete decoder and a complete encoder. Each frame of the video stream is decoded completely and a wide range of operations can be performed on the raw pixels, which leads to great flexibility of this architecture. However, this approach has a high complexity because the whole decoding and encoding procedure needs to be processed. Additionally, the information that is already available from the previous encoding such as the motion vectors of each frame should be reused for transcoding instead of being recomputed, to enhance the produced quality of the video.

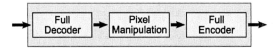

Figure 2.9: Cascaded pixel domain transcoder (CPDT)

2.4 Compressed Domain Video Transcoding

Based on the cascaded pixel domain transcoder (CPDT), several fast transcoding architectures that partly or completely avoid the decoding process have been proposed in the literature. If the decoding of the video stream is avoided, this kind of video adaptation is called compressed domain video transcoding. The field of compressed domain video transcoding has been explored in several recent studies, each of which focuses on a different specialized transcoding technique. A comprehensive overview of the research area dealing with these transcoding techniques is given by Vetro et al. in [35] as well as by Sun et al. in [36]. In this section we give an overview of the most important compressed domain transcoding techniques presented in the literature.

Due to its complexity, the CPDT architecture is not optimally suitable for real-time video adaptation. Therefore, it is necessary to reduce the number of decoding steps needed so that the video stream will not be decoded completely. Many video codecs, including those which we focus on in this work, use a mathematical function to transform the pixel values into the frequency domain to take advantage of the frequency distribution within blocks of pixels. Most video coding standards such as MPEG video use the DCT to transform each block from the pixel domain into the frequency domain. In a CPDT this transformation needs to be performed twice. Figure 2.10 schematically shows the building blocks of a CPDT that is able to adapt the detail dimension by recomputing the quantization of an incoming video stream. Firstly, the variable length coding needs to be inverted, which is indicated by the module VLC^{-1}, before the DCT values can be dequantized, which is depicted as Q^{-1}. Afterwards, the dequantized DCT values need to be transformed from the frequency domain into the pixel domain, which is illustrated as DCT^{-1}. The motion compensation module MC then recomputes the unpredicted frame for inter-coded frames. Now, the pixels of the frame may be manipulated and afterwards encoded again.

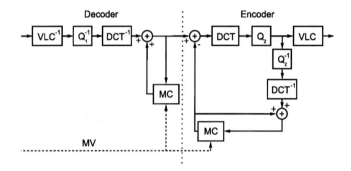

Figure 2.10: Pixel domain requantization transcoder

The transformation from the frequency domain into the pixel domain and back again consumes a great amount of processing power. The computation of the DCT may consume up to 30% of the processor cycles needed for the decoding process of digital video. Thus, avoiding the computation of the DCT can significantly reduce the processing power needed for video transcoding. Mathematically, the DCT is a linear and orthogonal transformation which is distributive with respect to matrix multiplications. To avoid the computation of the DCT, we can take advantage of these characteristics of the DCT [37]: To manipulate a block of pixels a, we need two matrices x and y to compute the altered block $b = x \cdot a \cdot y$. Due to the linearity of the DCT we have:

$$DCT(b) = DCT(x \cdot a \cdot y) = DCT(x) \cdot DCT(a) \cdot DCT(y) = X \cdot A \cdot Y$$

Thus, we can realize every linear pixel manipulation in the frequency domain by computing the corresponding manipulation matrices X and Y in the frequency domain. These matrices can be precomputed for different operations and therefore do not introduce any processing overhead at adaptation time. However, only I-frames are completely intra-coded and can be manipulated directly. For most other frames in digital video streams, the DCT values are not directly available because they are inter-coded, and do only contain residual errors resulting from the motion compensation mechanisms.

2.4.1 Compressed Domain Motion Compensation

To be able to alter a motion compensated block in the frequency domain the inverse motion compensation (IMC) needs to be computed. A method to perform the motion compensation in the compressed domain (DCT-MC) was firstly presented by Chang and Messerschmitt [37]. As a motion vector may point to an arbitrary position in the reference frame, the reference block does not necessarily lie on block boundaries, as illustrated in figure 2.11. In the pixel domain, this is uncomplicated, as the pixel values are directly accessible from the neighboring blocks. In the compressed domain, however, the DCT values of such a block B' are not directly available and need to be computed from up to four covering blocks B_i.

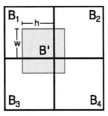

Figure 2.11: Arbitrary reference block

In the pixel domain, a block b' can be directly extracted by masking those parts of the four covering blocks $b_1, ..., b_4$:

$$b' = \sum_{i=1}^{4} h_{1i} b_i h_{2i} \qquad (2.13)$$

with

$$h_{11} = h_{13} = u_h = \begin{bmatrix} 0 & I_h \\ 0 & 0 \end{bmatrix}, h_{12} = h_{14} = u_{8-h},$$

$$h_{21} = h_{23} = l_w = \begin{bmatrix} 0 & 0 \\ I_w & 0 \end{bmatrix}, h_{22} = h_{24} = l_{8-w}$$

and I_h, I_w being identity matrices with $0 \leq h, w \leq 8$. The lower case notation indicates that this is computed in the pixel domain. By using equation (2.13) we get in the frequency domain:

$$B' = DCT(b') = DCT(\sum_{i=1}^{4} h_{1i} b_i h_{2i}) = \sum_{i=1}^{4} DCT(h_{1i}) B_i DCT(h_{2i}).$$

As already mentioned, these DCT matrices $DCT(h_{ij})$ can be precomputed and do not introduce any computational overhead at adaptation time. Merhav and Bhaskaran additionally proposed to use a decomposition of the used matrices and thereby reduced the number of operations needed up to 50% [38]. Further optimizations were proposed by Song and Yeo [39] as well as by Liu and Bovik [40]. Patil and Kumar recently proposed to aggregate neighboring macro blocks with common motion vectors and to process them as one big block [41]. By this approach, the number of operations, which are needed for the DCT-MC, are reduced by more than 80% compared to the original method proposed by Chang and Messerschmitt.

2.4.2 Requantization Transcoders

One way to reduce the bit rate of multimedia streams is to increase the quantizer scale value used during the encoding process of the video. This kind of transcoding is especially useful for mobile clients with wireless access because of the varying bandwidth of wireless connections. The easiest way to build a requantization transcoder is the open loop transcoder illustrated in figure 2.12. This approach can be computed very fast, as only the inverse quantization with the old quantizer scale value and the quantization with the new value are performed by this transcoder. Compared to the CPDT, not only the computation of the DCT but also the motion compensation loops are avoided. The produced quality of this transcoder, however, is rather poor because the introduced transcoding error is quite high. The reason for that is that a quantization with a higher quantizer scale value changes the encoded residual error of each block, which results in an error when reconstructing the frame at the decoder. Due to the motion compensation, the introduced reconstruction error accumulates until the next key frame while decoding consecutive frames.

Transcoder

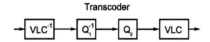

Figure 2.12: Open loop requantization transcoder

This effect of an accumulated reconstruction error is also called drift error and can be avoided by recomputing the encoded residual errors based on the new quantizer scale value in a so-called drift error loop. Assuncao et al. showed that the CPDT, which does not produce any drift error, can be reduced to a DCT domain transcoder, where all operations are performed in the DCT domain [42]. They demonstrated that the motion compensation loops of the original CPDT (see figure 2.10) can be combined into one single drift free loop. Additionally, the inverse operation of the DCT can be eliminated by using the compressed domain motion compensation (DCT-MC). These modifications result in the DCT domain requantization transcoder that is shown in figure 2.13. Within the drift free loop of this transcoder, the transcoding error that is introduced by the new quantization process, i.e., the difference between the original DCT values and the newly dequantized values, is removed from the original residual error.

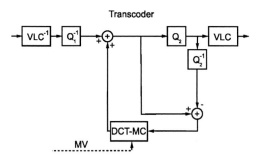

Figure 2.13: DCT domain requantization transcoder

By additionally using approximate matrices when computing the compressed domain motion compensation, the computational complexity of the transcoder presented by Assuncao et al. is reduced by 81% compared to the CPDT. Although their proposed transcoder is mathematically equivalent to the CPDT, the linear combination of the decoding and encoding loops causes minor arithmetic inaccuracies due to the non-linear nature of the quantization process within the loops. These inaccuracies, however, have no remarkable effect on the quality of the transcoded video [42] and can be ignored.

2.4.3 Frame Skipping Transcoders

The above-mentioned bit rate adaptation always reduces the overall quality of the transcoded video. In some cases, however, it may be desirable to retain the quality of each transmitted video frame while reducing the frame rate of a video stream. In this case, a frame-skipping transcoder which regularly or dynamically skips single input frames could be used. Different cases can be distinguished. The easiest case is skipping all frames that are not referenced by other frames, such as B-frames because those frames can be dropped by the transcoder without any influence on any of the remaining frames. However, B-frames also consume the smallest amount of bandwidth of a stream and therefore, it may be necessary to skip other frames as well. In the case of P-frames, frame-skipping would lead to invalid motion vectors of non-skipped frames because they may refer to a skipped frame.

Figure 2.14 illustrates a situation where a frame $t - 1$, which is used as reference frame by frame t, is selected for skipping. After skipping the frame, the motion vector v_t^1 of the macro block MB_t^1 becomes invalid and a new vector $\tilde{v}_t^1$ needs to be found. The block B_{t-1} to which the vector v_t^1 points is not available any more in the compressed

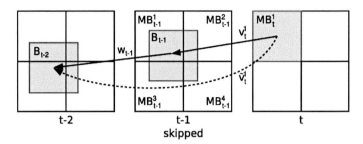

Figure 2.14: Frame skipping of motion compensated frames

domain, and therefore also the vector w_{t-1} is not available. Hwang et al. proposed to calculate the missing motion vector w_{t-1} by bilinear interpolation of the motion vectors of MB^i_{t-1} [43]. However, in the case of divergent motion vectors, i.e., vectors pointing into completely different directions, bilinear interpolation produces unsuitable motion vectors. Youn et al. therefore presented the forward dominant vector selection (FDVS) [44] which approximates the missing vector w_{t-1} by selecting a dominant vector. The dominant vector of a block is the motion vector of that macro block which has the biggest overlapping with the missing block. In the situation shown in figure 2.14, this would be the motion vector of MB^1_{t-1}. FDVS produces better results than bilinear interpolation in case of divergent motion vectors and does not need to compute any interpolation. Only in the case of similar sized overlapping regions, the FDVS may select an unsuitable motion vector. For such cases, Chen et al. proposed an activity dominant vector selection (ADVS) [45] which additionally takes into account the activity, i.e., the number of non-zero DCT values, of the corresponding macro blocks. Based on these mechanisms, Fung et al. proposed a frame-skipping transcoder which completely performs in the DCT domain [46, 47, 48]. This transcoder can save up to 60% of the processing time needed for the pixel domain approach [48].

2.4.4 Spatial Downscaling Transcoders

The above-mentioned transcoding approaches are mainly targeting the problem of bandwidth restrictions of mobile devices. Other often limited resources of mobile devices are their display size and their resolution. Additionally, most mobile devices do not have enough processing power to reduce the spatial resolution of a video stream by itself. To enable these devices to access high resolution video streams at all, the streams have to be downscaled before being transmitted to the client. Several different techniques that deal with spatial resolution downscaling within the DCT domain were proposed in recent papers. Shanableh and Ghanbari distinguished three main classes of different approaches [49]: averaging, filtering, and DCT decimation.

The simplest method is pixel averaging, where one downscaled pixel is computed by averaging the values of a group of incoming pixels. For downscaling by a factor of two, the averaging can be achieved by computing the bilinear interpolation for each frame. In the pixel domain, the bilinear interpolation b' of four neighboring blocks b_i can be expressed as follows:

$$b' = \sum_{i=1}^{4} h_{1i} b_i h_{2i}$$

with

$$h_{11} = h_{12} = h_{21}^t = h_{23}^t = \begin{bmatrix} q_{4\times8} \\ 0_{4\times8} \end{bmatrix},$$

$$h_{13} = h_{14} = h_{22}^t = h_{24}^t = \begin{bmatrix} 0_{4\times8} \\ q_{4\times8} \end{bmatrix},$$

and

$$q_{4\times8} = \begin{bmatrix} \frac{1}{2} & \frac{1}{2} & 0 & 0 & 0 & 0 & 0 & 0 \\ 0 & 0 & \frac{1}{2} & \frac{1}{2} & 0 & 0 & 0 & 0 \\ 0 & 0 & 0 & 0 & \frac{1}{2} & \frac{1}{2} & 0 & 0 \\ 0 & 0 & 0 & 0 & 0 & 0 & \frac{1}{2} & \frac{1}{2} \end{bmatrix}, \text{ and a } 4 \times 8 \text{ zero matrix } 0_{4\times8}.$$

Due to the linearity of the DCT, this computation can also be transferred into the frequency domain:

$$B' = \sum_{i=1}^{4} DCT(h_{1i} b_i h_{2i}) = \sum_{i=1}^{4} DCT(h_{1i}) DCT(b_i) DCT(h_{2i}) = \sum_{i=1}^{4} H_{1i} B_i H_{2i}$$

Similar to the matrices in the compressed domain motion compensation, the static matrices H_{1i} and H_{2i} can be precomputed. However, the matrices h_{1i} and h_{2i} are sparse matrices and therefore, their corresponding matrices in the frequency domain, i.e., H_{1i} and H_{2i}, are dense, which results in a high computational overhead. This overhead was reduced by Merhav and Bhaskaran by exploiting the special structure of the involved matrices [38].

The second class of approaches for spatial downscaling, as identified by Shanableh and Ghanbari, are filtering approaches [49]. Yin et al. proposed a filtering approach that uses frequency synthesis to transform four incoming 8×8 pixels blocks into one 8×8 pixels block [50]. Another filtering approach for downscaling digital images and videos with an arbitrary ratio has recently been proposed by Yu et al. [51]. Their approach does not use any multiplication, which reduces the complexity. Roma and Sousa argued that filtering approaches like these may be regarded to be equivalent to the aforementioned averaging approaches. They presented their arbitrary downscaling algorithm which uses a filtering approach in [52].

The third class of spatial downscaling approaches are DCT decimation algorithms that use only a reduced number of DCT values for the downscaling process. Shanableh and Ghanbari proposed an approach, that uses the upper left 4×4 DCT-values of each four neighboring blocks B_i [49]. These values are transferred into the pixel domain by computing the corresponding inverse 4×4 DCT, and then form a new 8×8 pixel block which is transferred back into the frequency domain by computing their DCT values. Based on this approach, Dugad and Ahuja proposed an approach which works completely in the DCT domain [53]. It produces visually better results, and can be computed much faster than the bilinear interpolation. Salazar and Tran extended their approach to arbitrary scaling factors but at higher computational costs [54]. Mukherjee and Mitra proposed yet another approach for arbitrary resizing of images in the frequency domain [55] which is also based on the approach of Dugad and Ahuja. They mainly improved the produced quality at similar computational costs. Lee and Lin proposed a generalized DCT decimation scheme which also reduces the computational costs and increases the produced quality [56].

One of the major problems in the context of video scaling is again the existence of dependencies between consecutive frames in the video streams. Thus, besides the downscaling of DCT values, also the motion vectors need to be downscaled and the residual blocks need to be updated. Lee et al. compared different solutions and showed that an activity-weighted median filtering (awmf) approach produced the best visual results [57]. The activity-weighted distance between each vector to all others is calculated as:

$$d_i = \frac{1}{ACT_i} \sum_{j=1, j \neq i}^{4} \|v_i - v_j\|$$

where the activity ACT_i of macro block i can be computed as the squared or absolute sum of DCT values, the number of non-zero DCT values or just the DC value of the macro block. Afterwards, the motion vector for the downscaled macro block is calculated as

$$v = \frac{1}{2} \arg \min_{v_i \in \{v_1, v_2, v_3, v_4\}} d_i$$

In the case of H.263, MPEG-4 or H.264 video, each macro block may contain up to four motion vectors, which is one motion vector per 8×8 pixels block. If the incoming macro blocks do not already contain four motion vectors each, this feature can be exploited for downscaling. In the case of downscaling by a factor of two, the four incoming vectors need to be downscaled and can be used directly for the four resulting 8×8 pixels block.

However, any changes to the motion vectors introduce certain transcoding errors, which leads to a visual quality degradation. Such transcoding errors can be reduced by a motion vector refinement in the pixel domain. Shen et al. introduced a transcoder architecture which takes this intro account and therefore partially uses computation in the pixel domain [58]. The spatial downscaling of DCT values is performed completely in the frequency domain, whereas motion vector refinement is achieved by approximating the original frames by firstly calculating the inverse DCT of the downscaled frame and secondly upscaling the frame within the pixel domain. The computational saving of this architecture is dependent on the transcoded video sequence and varies between 25% and 75% compared to video downscaling in the pixel domain [58].

2.5 Video Adaptation Architectures

In our work we concentrated on video adaptation for mobile devices. Due to the limited resources of such devices, the adaptation will not be performed on the devices themselves but on some other nodes that are involved in the communication process. In the literature one can find several different systems that provide some kind of video adaptation to their devices such as in [59, 60] or in [61]. The proposed systems can be classified by the number of nodes involved in the adaptation process. Single node systems consist of one single node each that provides video adaptation in the network. Communication between two of these systems is not intended. Multi node systems consist of several, not necessarily different, nodes in the network. These systems can be subdivided into systems where the video adaptation is achieved on one single node only and systems where the adaptation is processed on multiple nodes. In this section we give an overview about various proposed systems of all three categories.

2.5.1 Single Node Systems

Amir et al. described an application level video gateway which is able to transcode Motion-JPEG videos to H.261 videos [62]. In [59] Vetro et al. presented their vision for media conversion to support mobile users. They proposed a requantization transcoding architecture which should be implemented at a single video gateway. Chi et al. used an existing web caching proxy implementation to build a transcoding system for web objects, including MPEG-4 videos [63]. As their system uses a web caching proxy, it only supports HTTP over TCP for data transport. A more multimedia-centric approach was described by Guo et al. [64], where active routers transcode multimedia streams during their transmission to the client. Lei and Georganas suggested a quite static implementation of a transcoding gateway in [65]. However, due to the use of non-standard protocols this approach only has a limited usability. A more standard-based and flexible proxy which combines adaptation techniques as well as caching capabilities in one proxy was proposed by Schojer et al. [66].

2.5.2 Multi Node Systems

One system consisting of multiple nodes was proposed by HP Research in [67, 68, 60]. It consists of transcoding nodes and management nodes. The latter ones are called portal nodes and they are responsible for selecting an appropriate transcoding node by contacting a central Service Location Manager. In contrast to each of the following systems, here the transcoding process takes place on a single transcoding node of the whole system. In [69] Hemy et al. proposed to implement filter capabilities on routers. Those routers should be able to adapt video streams by frame dropping if congestion occurs. Mao et al. presented in [70] a system consisting of several adaptation nodes by which a video stream can be adapted. But before any transcoding can take place, the complete adaptation path from the source to the client needs to be determined and configured with their system. A more adaptive approach was presented by Hashimoto and Shibata in [71, 61, 72] where a middleware that is based on mechanism known from the Java Media Framework[2] was proposed. An approach based on active networking technology was proposed by Duysburgh et al. in [73, 74] where active nodes build a multicast tree and some of these nodes can transcode video streams.

2.6 Video Quality Measurement

When dealing with video coding or with video adaptation a naturally arising topic is the measurement of the produced quality. The quality of a video sequence depends on several different subjective and objective aspects which, unfortunately, cannot always be well defined. The interests of a viewer as well as his or her experience with digital video, for instance, may heavily influence his or her subjective quality impression [75]. Thus, the most accurate method to measure the quality of a video stream is the usage of experiments that evaluate subjective, user-specific reactions to the quality of video streams.

However, qualitative research methods such as subjective tests, for instance, are very time-consuming which limits their practicability. To avoid such costly experiments, one can use objective quality metrics instead. Objective quality metrics are designed to rate the quality of video streams without performing subjective tests. A well-known objective quality metric for compressed still images and digital videos that is widely used in the research community, is the peak signal to noise ratio (PSNR). The PSNR is a logarithmic representation of the mean squared error (MSE) between the compressed image and its corresponding reference image. The MSE between an image Q and its reference image P, with $m \times n$ pixels each, is defined as:

$$MSE = \frac{1}{mn} \sum_{i=0}^{m-1} \sum_{j=0}^{n-1} ||P(i,j) - Q(i,j)||^2,$$

---

[2]http://java.sun.com/javase/technologies/desktop/media/jmf/index.jsp

and the PSNR is defined as:

$$PSNR = 10 \log_{10} \left(\frac{MAX^2}{MSE} \right)$$

where MAX is the maximum value of a pixel, which usually is 255. For video streams, the PSNR values are computed for every frame and can be averaged for the whole stream. For color images and color videos, the PSNR values are computed for each color component separately. The most important component is the luminance as the human perception is more sensitive to the luminance component than to the chrominance components. Therefore, it is usually sufficient to use only the PSNR values of the luminance component for quality measurements of digital video. In the context of lossy compression techniques, typical PSNR values for video frames range between 20 and 45 decibel (dB), where higher values stand for a better quality. Video streams which are encoded at the highest possible bit rate with a current video codec usually reach PSNR values around 40 dB.

In the research community, PSNR is quite popular because it is well understood by researchers and easy to compute. However, using PSNR as a metric for the quality of digital video still has certain drawbacks because it is computed byte-by-byte for each single frame. The motion between consecutive frames of a video stream, for instance, is not covered by the PSNR values. Additionally, some studies with still images show that the PSNR values do not always correlate with the subjective quality of compressed images [76]. This also results to the fact that higher PSNR values indeed reflect a closer similarity of the compressed frames and the reference frames, but not necessarily a higher quality perceived by a human viewer. Nevertheless, Huynh-Thu and Ghanbari recently investigated the scope of validity of the PSNR metric for image and video quality assessment [77]. By comparing the average PSNR values of different test sequences with their corresponding subjective quality, they showed that the PSNR values highly correlate with subjective quality results for video sequences with the same content. Thus, PSNR is a valid metric when comparing the quality of a given video sequence encoded with different codecs or with different encoding parameters. In sum, for our research purposes PSNR can be used as an objective quality metric to evaluate different transcoding features and mechanisms as long as we compare the PSNR values computed for different versions of the same video stream. However, due to the content-dependencies a cross-video comparison is not possible. When comparing the PSNR values of different video streams, i.e., streams with different content, the results may differ from those achieved by subjective quality assessment.

Another problem of PSNR is that it can only be computed for video streams with the same frame rate and spatial resolution as the reference frames. If either the spatial or the temporal resolution of a video stream differs from those of the reference stream, the computation of the PSNR values needs to be adapted correspondingly. In general, there are two possibilities to compute the PSNR in these situations: either the decoded frames are adapted to the same resolution as the reference frames or vice versa. In the literature, however, it is often not mentioned how exactly the researchers computed the presented PSNR values. Only the presented PSNR values may indicate how they were computed. In this work, we use the conventions, which can also be found in several major publications in this context, such as [43, 49, 78, 50, 56]: The spatial resolution is adapted to the resolution of the reference stream and the PSNR values are only computed for those frames which are present in both streams.

2.7 Summary

In this chapter, we have presented background information on digital video coding, streaming, and adaptation. In particular, we gave an overview of important video coding standards and presented the most important video coding techniques that are used by the majority of video coding standards. Afterwards we have provided information on video adaptation in general, including the introduction of different adaptation dimensions. We have presented how scalable video coding might solve the problem of supporting the great heterogeneity of mobile devices. Nevertheless, single layer video adaptation still is a key technology for adaptive video streaming. Single layer video streams are characterized by a lower complexity needed for their encoding and decoding compared to multi layer video streams. Additionally, each video layer in a layered video stream introduces a certain encoding and transmission overhead, which limits the reasonable number of layers. The limited number of layers also lowers the variety of possible adaptations. This makes the use of single layer video in combination with compressed domain transcoding more flexible in terms of adaptation granularity. Additionally, most video streams on the Internet today as well as in digital television or digital entertainment systems are encoded as single layer video streams. This prominence of single layer video streams additionally emphasizes the need for single layer video adaptation. Therefore, we have presented detailed information on compressed domain transcoding mechanisms as the base technologies for single layer video adaptation in this chapter.

However, almost all of the approaches presented in the literature limit their focus on the adaptation of video streams in only one single dimension. There are approaches that solely reduce the temporal resolution of a stream such as those presented in [44] and [48]. Other approaches that reduce the spatial resolution of each frame were presented, for instance, in [38], [51] and [56]. An approach that solely reduces the detail resolution of a video stream by performing a requantization can, for instance, be found in [42]. Only very few approaches take into account a second or even third adaptation dimension. The most comprehensive approach was presented by Shanableh and Ghanbari in [49]. However, they treated each adaptation dimension separately and neglected how these mechanisms can be combined smartly.

In addition to the presented adaptation mechanisms discussed in the research literature, we have also outlined different proposed architectures that provide video adaptation services to mobile clients. In summary, however, an integrated approach for multidimensional video transcoding that caters for the specific and complex demands of mobile devices has not yet been proposed. This is the focus of our approach that we introduce in the following chapters. In the next chapter we present our multimedia gateway architecture that provides video adaptation services to mobile clients. A discussion of multidimensional video adaptation as well as our multidimensional transcoding approach are presented afterwards in chapter 4.

Chapter 3

Multimedia Gateway Architecture

One important aspect in the context of adaptive video streaming is the place for processing the video adaptation. Considering that a video is streamed from a server to a proxy and from this proxy to a client, there are three different network nodes that may process the adaptation of the video stream, i.e., adaptation at the server, at the intermediate proxy or at the client. Adaptation at the client side is usually not an option because of the limited resources at the client. Additionally, the wireless network connection should, if possible, not be overloaded by video streams with high bit rates. Thus, two different approaches for providing an adaptation service to mobile devices can be distinguished: a server-based approach and a proxy-based approach. In the first solution, an adaptation service is implemented on the same machine as the multimedia server, whereas in the second one it is implemented on an intermediate proxy machine.

A server-based solution provides quite limited flexibility because the adaptation service is only available for those streams which are hosted on multimedia servers that implement such adaptation capabilities. Yet, it would reduce the network load during transmission of the stream on the complete path from the server to the client because the bit rate of the video stream has already been reduced before being sent over the network. Additionally, a server-based solution would allow the adaptation process to access more information about the video that is not contained in the encoded stream. An example of such additional information is meta data about the stream which is possibly available at the media server but not at other nodes such as a proxy.

In a proxy-based solution only the media stream itself can be used for adaptation. This solution, however, provides the most flexibility because a client which needs an adaptation service in order to receive and display a certain multimedia stream could get a properly tailored stream from every reachable server by using the adaptation proxy. Another advantage of a proxy-based adaptation service is that it can be located closer to the client, and therefore closer to the communication's bottleneck, which typically is the wireless connection. This gives the adaptation process the ability to react more quickly to the varying available network bandwidth of the client's device.

In our work we favor a proxy-based solution due to its higher flexibility to provide video adaptation services to mobile clients. For this approach, several multimedia gateways should be installed in the access network of mobile devices, as described in our target scenario in section 1.2. The main functionality of such a gateway is to serve as an RTSP/RTP proxy so that a client may request a media stream from the proxy instead of connecting directly to the corresponding media server. Hence, we designed and implemented an RTSP/RTP proxy system with the name *Beaver*. Besides the proxy functionality, we included further features in the implementation such as stream reflection, gateway discovery, capability exchange, session transfer and cooperative caching, which will be described in this chapter. The core feature of our multimedia gateway system is, however, a video adaptation service for mobile devices. This central topic of our work will be presented in detail in chapter 4.

The rest of this chapter is organized as follows: Based on our target scenario, section 3.1 presents some basic requirements for the gateway design. Section 3.2 describes the core design issues of our gateway system. Afterwards, we describe the actual prototype implementation of our multimedia gateway in section 3.3, before we conclude this chapter with a summary in section 3.4.

3.1 Requirements

A multimedia gateway system that is located in an access network may enhance the service quality for mobile clients by providing video adaptation services. As already mentioned in section 1.2, we derived the following requirements that have to be considered for such a multimedia gateway system:

(1) Video streams can be tailored to the requirements of the receiving client which are defined by the capabilities of the mobile device as well as the user's preferences;

(2) Different adaptation techniques should be available at the adaptation system to satisfy the demands of different users and devices;

(3) The adaptation system should be transparent from the user's perspective;

(4) The mobility of the users should be supported by the adaptation system;

(5) The system should be interoperable with existing streaming solutions.

Figure 3.1 depicts the target scenario that was described in the introduction of this thesis, for one single gateway. On the left side one can see different video sources which are available on the Internet. The servers on the left illustrate different media servers that provide pre-recorded content on the Internet such as traditional video-on-demand services (VoD) do. The video camera illustrates a live source which provides live video streams, for instance, produced at sports events. In the middle of the figure one can find

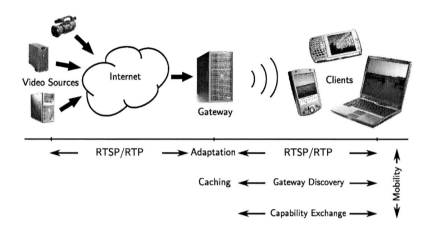

Figure 3.1: Multimedia gateway overview

the gateway which is connected to the Internet and can be reached from wireless clients. This gateway acts as an RTSP/RTP proxy on the application layer and provides video adaptation services to its clients. Additionally, this gateway could be equipped with some caching functionalities to reduce the load between the access network and the Internet. By supporting different adaptation techniques on the gateway, requirements (1) and (2) can already be satisfied.

A client which would like to use the adaptation service on a gateway needs to know how to address the gateway. Therefore, a gateway discovery mechanism is needed for the clients to discover available multimedia gateways. When a client requests to use the adaptation services provided by a gateway, this gateway needs to get some information about the requirements of the device as well as the user's preferences in order to chose a suitable adaptation mechanism and parameters. Therefore, some capability exchange mechanism is needed as indicated in the figure. By providing a gateway discovery mechanism as well as a mechanism for capability exchange that work both without user interaction, a gateway system can fulfill the requirement (3). The capability exchange is also needed for requirements (1) and (2). The last aspect that is shown in the figure is the mobility of the devices. Due to its mobility, a client device may reach the communication range of another gateway, which may be more suitable, for instance, due to a lower communication delay. Therefore, some hand-over mechanisms between the two different gateways are needed as also requested in requirement (4). By using IETF standard protocols for signaling and data transport, we can satisfy requirement (5), although a legacy client may not be able to benefit from all proposed features.

3.2 Design Issues

We designed our multimedia gateway architecture so that it fulfills the aforementioned requirements. In chapter 2.2, we already presented the core aspects of video streaming over the Internet by using the IETF protocols RTSP and RTP. RTSP is used for signaling purposes, whereas RTP is used for data transport. The main reason for this separation is the need for asynchronous operation of both communication aspects. Neither should any signaling messages interrupt the data transport, nor should the data packets interfere any signaling messages. Additionally, the signaling messages are usually sent reliably by using TCP at transport layer, whereas the data packets are typically sent unreliably by using UDP. We used this concept of separation between signaling and data transport as a core design concept for our multimedia gateway.

Figure 3.2 shows the overall architecture and the main components of our multimedia gateway. In the upper part of the architecture one can find the components of the control path, which handles the RTSP messages that the gateway exchanges with the media servers as well as with the requesting clients. Below the dashed line in the figure, one can find the data path which is responsible for handling the RTP packets arriving from a server and forwarding them to the corresponding clients. As indicated in the figure, our gateway system supports several clients and servers. Most of the internal components such as the `ServerRTSP` as well as the `ClientRTSP` relate to exactly one server or client connection and are therefore instantiated for each connected server and client. However, for the sake of simplicity, figure 3.2 shows the internal components of our gateway system only once.

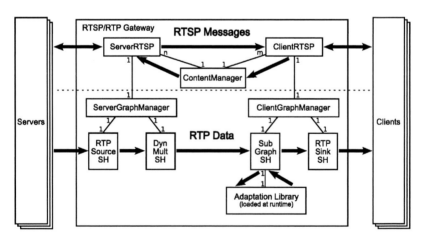

Figure 3.2: Multimedia gateway architecture

3.2.1 Data Path

For data processing we use the concept of stream handlers (SHs) as introduced by Herrtwich and Wolf [79]. SHs are small data processing units which can be connected into an acyclic directed data path by a controlling unit. A SH can either consume or generate data units or transmit data units from its input to its output. Additionally, each SH can manipulate the processed data units. When several SHs are connected to a data path, a stream can be processed and manipulated within the data path in a certain manner. The controlling unit which connects several SHs to form a data path, is called graph manager (GM). The GM is responsible for the configuration of each SH when the data path is built as well as for its control and reconfiguration during the transmission of the stream. In figure 3.2 one can see, for instance, a server graph manager that controls two SHs. These SHs process incoming RTP packets and forwards them to the connected SH.

3.2.2 Decoupled Client and Server Side

Additionally to the horizontal separation of control path and data path, there is also a vertical separation in our gateway design. Each gateway needs to be able to handle several client connections as well as several server connections. If several different clients like to consume the same media stream, our gateway architecture provides, if necessary, each client with its individually tailored video stream, while using one single server connection. Therefore, we decoupled the server side connections from the client side connections within the gateway. The relationships between both sides are handled in one central component that is called `ContentManager`. The `ContentManager` of our gateway architecture takes care of all active server-client connections.

This decoupled client and server side connections facilitate the proxy to act as a flexible reflector, which is one of the key functionalities of our RTSP/RTP proxy as we presented in [5]. A reflector can serve several clients that request the same content, by using solely one shared unicast or multicast server connection. This reflector can, for instance, be used for application layer multicast to save network traffic in the case of live media streaming. Here some live content would be streamed simultaneously to several clients. Another example of a use case for the reflector is collaborative media streaming, where a group of users collaboratively receive the same content, as we described in [4].

3.2.3 Extendable Data Path

As mentioned before, the core functionality of our multimedia gateway is to provide video adaptation services to mobile clients. Thus, the gateway needs to be able to use some adaptation methods which can be applied to the video streams. If a video stream is requested by a client via the RTSP/RTP proxy all data packets of this stream are handled by the SHs in the data path of the proxy. Thus, it seemed only natural to integrate video adaptation process directly into the data path. We also integrated the ability to extend the data path of the gateway dynamically, as the heterogeneity of mobile devices in combination with different video formats may necessitate different adaptation mechanisms. The so-called `SubGraphSH`, as shown in figure 3.2, may load an adaptation library at runtime of the proxy and integrate it into the client side of the current data path. This extends the current data path, and each packet that is received from the media server is additionally processed by the adaptation library and thereby adapted to the requirements of the client. The library has to implement the `SubGraphSH` interface so that it can be integrated into the data path.

As the adaptation library can be loaded at runtime, the proxy can use several different adaptation libraries according to the needed adaptation methods. Based on the available information about both the requested media stream and the requesting client, the `ClientGraphManager` causes the `SubGraphSH` to load a suitable library accordingly.

3.3 Implementation

Based on the aforementioned considerations about the design of our gateway architecture we implemented an RTSP/RTP proxy that can be used as a multimedia gateway for video adaptation, as we presented in [6]. This implementation is called *Beaver* and was also used in another project, dealing with collaborative streaming, as presented by Kahmann in [80, 81].

For RTP and RTCP communication we used a third party library that is called ccRTP and is part of the GNU project[1]. This library provides an easy to use interface and internally uses one thread for data communication. All other components of the gateway were implemented from scratch following a single-threaded model. The following subsections describe different important features and aspects of the implementation.

3.3.1 Stream Reflection

Video reflectors in general are intermediate systems that fetch a video stream from a remote source and provide the stream to their typically local clients. Such reflectors are useful in those situation when a client cannot directly access a certain media stream from a remote source. If, for instance, a media stream is distributed in a multicast session, a client in a non-multicast capable network may connect to a reflector which maps the multicast session to an individual unicast session for the requesting client. Another example is the situation that a multicast capable client cannot decode a media stream that is distributed in a multicast session because the client, for instance, does not support the encoding format of the stream. Then, a reflector that is capable of adapting the media stream may provide the client with an adapted stream in a separate unicast session. Thus, a reflector may share one single server session among several client

---

[1]http://www.gnu.org/software/ccrtp/

sessions as illustrated in figure 3.3. We call these client sessions together with the shared server session a reflector session, which a client may leave or join dynamically.

The decoupled client and server sides, as described in section 3.2.2, enable the proxy to dynamically connect several client side data paths to one single server side data path and thereby build a reflector session. When several clients should receive the same media stream by using our gateway, the data packets need to be copied for each client. Therefore, we implemented a special SH which is able to transfer each incoming data packet to several connected SHs. The name of this SH is DynMultSH as it dynamically multiplies each incoming packet according to the connected SHs. Instead of copying each data packet for each connected client, the reference of the packet is forwarded to the client side data paths, by the DynMultSH. Therefore, we are using a so-called shared pointer from the Boost libraries[2] that internally uses a reference counter to keep track of all objects referencing the packet.

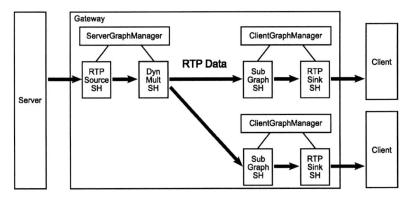

Figure 3.3: Reflector session with two clients

If a client joins an existing reflector session, its corresponding data path within the gateway will be connected to the corresponding DynMultSH of the server side data path, and the client will receive the data packets. Figure 3.3 shows an example of a reflector session with two connected clients that receive the same content from one single server. If a client in a reflector session requests to pause the stream and therefore leaves the reflector session, its data path will simply be disconnected from the corresponding server side data path. If this client wants to resume the stream later on or requests another stream, the gateway will set up a new server session and create an individual server side data path to which the client side data path will be connected. Similar to the situation that a client joins an existing reflector session, a client that has left the reflector session earlier may also join the reflector session again.

---

[2]http://www.boost.org

As each connected client gets its individual client side data path within our gateway implementation, the client can also benefit from the extendable data path. As illustrated in figure 3.2, the client side data path may be extended by loading an adaptation library at runtime and therefore, each client within a reflector session may receive an individually adapted media stream. This concept could also be easily extended to support the loading of an adaptation library at the server side data path to provide several clients with the same tailored stream.

3.3.2 Gateway Discovery

Before a client can use any adaptation service that is provided by a multimedia gateway, it needs to know how to address the gateway. In a static environment, this could be easily achieved by some kind of static configuration. In a dynamic environment with mobile clients, a more flexible solution is needed. Therefore, we designed a discovery mechanism which enables a client to automatically find an appropriate gateway, either by actively searching a gateway or by passively listening to gateway announcements.

The problem of gateway discovery is similar to the problem of service location in local area networks. This problem is addressed by several well-known service discovery mechanisms as described, for instance, by Richard in [82]. All well-known service location mechanisms are based on a reactive service discovery paradigm, i.e., a client requests a service whenever it is needed. This may be an appropriate solution for static service environments, but for mobile devices a more proactive approach similar to the one proposed by Bechler et al. [83] is needed. The advantage of a proactive approach is a reduced overhead for higher number of clients in the network. In the case of gateway discovery, the number of clients typically is several times higher than the number of gateways in the network. Therefore, the overhead introduced by service requests that are sent actively by the clients is higher compared to the overhead introduced by service announcements sent by the gateways. With the proactive approach, however, the startup delay before a service could firstly be used is increased because the client may need to wait for the next service announcement. Therefore, we propose to use a hybrid approach that combines the proactive and the reactive approach. Following this idea our service environment benefits from a lower overhead of the proactive approach while at the same time provides only a small startup delay by additionally using reactive service requests.

A well-known service discovery protocol is the Service Location Protocol (SLP) [84] defined by the IETF. SLP defines three different components that are called agents: Service agents (SA) propagate information about a service including its address and its characteristics. Directory agents (DA) optionally implement a service directory to improve the scalability of SLP. With the existence of a DA all SAs have to register their services at the DA. The third component is the user agent (UA) which is responsible for finding an appropriate service in the network for a requesting application. If a DA is available in the network, the UA sends its requests to the DA or to a well-defined multicast address otherwise. In the latter case, all SA listen to the well-defined multicast address and therefore may react on service requests sent by UAs.

For our multimedia gateway system, we designed a gateway discovery mechanism based on SLP which uses reactive service requests sent by the clients as well as proactive service announcements sent by the gateways. All gateways in the network implement a SA that answers service requests and periodically sends service announcements. The clients, on the other hand, implement a UA that listens to these service announcements from the gateways and additionally may send service requests if needed. Thus, with this approach, all gateways periodically send service announcements to all clients in the network, and the clients may additionally send service requests whenever they need to discover a new gateway. A client that would like to use a multimedia gateway may either wait for a service announcement from a nearby gateway or actively send a service request to which every nearby gateway may react to. As the service announcements are sent periodically, the client will learn about the existence of other gateways in its surrounding. The service announcements as well as the service requests are both sent to well-defined multicast addresses.

Due to the fact that the usability of a gateway is topologically bound, we limit the range of service announcements by using a low time to live (TTL) for these messages. The appropriate value of the TTL depends on the number of available gateways in the access network. Every time a client reaches the domain of a gateway which is defined by the TTL of the announcement messages, it will notice its existence and can check its suitability. If, for instance, the conditions of the communication channel between client and gateway such as delay, jitter or bandwidth decline, it may be worthwhile to transfer the session to another gateway. However, the suitability of a gateway is not only limited by the conditions of the communication channel but also by its current load and available transcoding mechanisms. Such information could also be embedded into the service announcement messages sent by the gateways.

3.3.3 Capability Exchange

Without video adaptation, content providers may support different devices by providing several versions of each video stream at different quality levels. In such a situation, a user needs to chose that version of the stream that fits best to the requirements of his or her device. We believe, however, that the user should be able to simply use an adaptation service without being bothered with any decisions about different coding formats or encoding parameters. Thus, we moved this decision from the user to the gateway: The gateway should chose an appropriate adaptation method to provide the most suitable version of the stream to the client. For this purpose the gateway needs some information about the client device as well as about the user preferences, which is achieved by the capability exchange mechanism that we integrated into our architecture.

Profile Description

For capability exchange, we created a profile description based on the Composite Capability/ Preference Profiles (CC/PP) [85]. CC/PP is a recommendation of the World Wide Web Consortium[3] (W3C) and allows a description of device capabilities as well as user preferences. CC/PP is based on the Resource Description Framework (RDF) [86], which was defined by the W3C for a description of metadata on the web.

A CC/PP profile has a 2-level hierarchy containing one or more components, which have one or more attributes each. Figure 3.4 shows a simple example of a CC/PP profile. The attributes of a profile describe the client capabilities for each component. For a description of the hardware of a device, a CC/PP profile may, for instance, define a component *Hardware*, which may contain attributes like *Processor, Memory* or *Display Resolution*. The CC/PP standard itself does not define any specific profile description. Therefore, we developed a basic profile description that can be used to chose an appropriate video adaptation mechanism at the gateway.

```
<?xml version="1.0" encoding="utf-8"?>
<rdf:RDF xmlns:rdf="http://www.w3.org/1999/02/22-rdf-syntax-ns#"
         xmlns:ccpp="http://www.w3.org/2002/11/08-ccpp-schema#"
         xmlns:beaver="http://www.ibr.cs.tu-bs.de/~brandt/media/beaver-s#">
  <rdf:Description rdf:ID="HP-HX2750-Pocket-PC">
    <ccpp:component>
      <rdf:Description rdf:ID="Hardware">
      <rdf:type rdf:resource="http://www.ibr.cs.tu-bs.de/~brandt/media/beaver-s#Hardware"/>
        <beaver:DisplayHeight>320</beaver:DisplayHeight>
        <beaver:DisplayWidth>240</beaver:DisplayWidth>
      </rdf:Description>
    </ccpp:component>
    <ccpp:component>
      <rdf:Description rdf:ID="Software">
      <rdf:type rdf:resource="http://www.ibr.cs.tu-bs.de/~brandt/media/beaver-s#Software"/>
        <beaver:OSName>Pocket PC 2003 se</beaver:OSName>
        <beaver:VideoFormats>
          <rdf:Seq>
            <rdf:li>video/mp4</rdf:li>
            <rdf:li>video/H263</rdf:li>
          </rdf:Seq>
        </beaver:VideoFormats>
      </rdf:Description>
    </ccpp:component>
    <ccpp:component>
      <rdf:Description rdf:ID="User">
      <rdf:type rdf:resource="http://www.ibr.cs.tu-bs.de/~brandt/media/beaver-s#User"/>
        <beaver:MinFrames>30</beaver:MinFrames>
        <beaver:MinVideoRate>2048</beaver:MinVideoRate>
      </rdf:Description>
    </ccpp:component>
  </rdf:Description>
</rdf:RDF>
```

Figure 3.4: Example of a simple client CC/PP profile

---

[3]http://www.w3c.org

This profile description contains four components: *Hardware, Software, User* and *Priority*. The component *Hardware* contains several attributes that describe the hardware of the client device such as CPU frequency, memory size, display height and display width. The component *Software* contains attributes which describe the software environment installed on the device such as the name and the version of the operating system as well as supported video formats. The component *User* allows a definition of user preferences and contains attributes like the preferred minimal bit rate for video streams or the minimal frame rate that the user is willing to accept. The fourth component is called *Priority* and may be used whenever some conflicting attributes exists. This component only contains one attribute called *Priorities* that may contain a list of key-value pairs that assigns certain attributes a priority in the range of 0 to 100. If, for instance, the minimal frame rate in combination with the minimum spatial resolution results in a video stream with a bit rate higher than the maximal bit rate that the device may receive, the priorities might give a hint whether to further reduce the frame rate or the spatial resolution. A very simple example of a client profile is given in figure 3.4. This profile defines the display resolution, the supported video formats as well as one user preference. A CC/PP schema that defines the complete profile can be found in appendix A.1.

Capability Exchange with RTSP

The signaling protocol of the gateway, RTSP, does currently not define any kind of capability exchange regarding the playback capabilities of the client. However, for this purpose we can use the possibility of RTSP to exchange general parameters. RTSP defines an optional method called SET_PARAMETER, which can be used to exchange any user-defined data between both parties of an RTSP session. The RTSP standard gives only a short example of how to use this method and defines that such "a request should only contain a single parameter to allow the client to determine why a particular request failed" [18]. Instead of exchanging each single attribute from the client profile in a separate RTSP message, the whole CC/PP profile can be embedded in the body of one single SET_PARAMETER message and can be sent from the requesting client to the gateway. As the gateway needs this information before the actual streaming can start, the client should send its profile between session setup and its first PLAY message. Any changes to the profile may also be sent from the client to the gateway afterwards, for instance, whenever as the user would like to change any preferences during the streaming session.

In the case that the gateway cannot understand some portions of the profile or if any attribute contains an invalid value, it will send a response message with a response code indicating an invalid parameter. This message also contains an error report, which the client can use to identify the invalid attribute. If a foreign gateway does not even recognize the profile at all, it will, according to the RTSP standard, simply response to the SET_PARAMETER message from the client with a response code indicating that this method is not supported.

3.3.4 Session Transfer

From the user's point of view, one of the main advantages of mobile devices is their mobility. Thus, a multimedia gateway that provides an adaptation service for mobile devices should support this mobility as far as possible. As we described in our target scenario in section 1.2, the multimedia gateways are located near the edge of the access network. Therefore, some hand-off mechanisms between neighboring gateways are needed. Roy et al. presented three different mechanisms for application level hand-off support for mobile media transcoding sessions in [87]. All three mechanisms need up to three different signaling messages between both gateways. As our gateway implementation uses RTSP for signaling purpose, we defined some new RTSP messages that can be used for session transfer according to the mechanisms described by Roy et al. A SESSION_TRANSFER message that includes information about the stream as well as the current offset, can be sent from the current gateway to the future gateway to initiate a session transfer. Now the new gateway can setup a media session with the corresponding media server. The SESSION_DATA message can be used to transfer partial state information from the current to the new gateway so that the new gateway can immediately start with video adaptation. Finally, the current gateway finishes the adaptation of the current frame. After sending this frame to the client, it sends a SESSION_SWITCH message to the new gateway, which then starts sending streaming data to the client. After this final message of the session transfer, the old gateway may stop its current RTSP session by sending a TEARDOWN to the server. This hand-off mechanism is called a two-stage hand-off with explicit switch (TSES) by Roy et al. The methods SESSION_DATA and SESSION_SWITCH may also be combined which leads to a method called single stage with explicit switching (SSES). The third method described by Roy et al. is called two-stage hand-off with implicit switching (TSIS). It completely avoids any switching message but uses implicit switching at a certain key frame later on in the remaining video stream.

The lowest switching delay was achieved by the ISIS method because no explicit switch message was used. The SSES method produced the highest delay. When using the SSES or the TSES method, the video stream that arrives at the client is completely identical compared to the situation without session transfer. With the ISIS method, however, it is possible that the client receives some data twice or that some data gets lost. Therefore, the stream that a client receives when ISIS is used might be different compared to a stream without session transfer. Due to these pros and cons of the proposed methods, we implemented only the TSES method in our gateway implementation.

3.3.5 Cooperative Caching

Although network capacities as well as the coding efficiency of digital video standards are constantly increasing, the high bit rates of digital video streams still consume large amounts of available network capacities. Caching mechanisms can be used to store multimedia objects on the gateways to reduce the network load between gateways and media servers. Due to the size of multimedia streams, several special caching strategies for multimedia objects are proposed in the literature such as prefix caching [88, 89], sliding interval caching [90, 91], and segment based caching [92, 93, 94]. With prefix caching, only the prefixes of popular video sequences are cached to reduce the start up delay for such video streams. With sliding interval caching, the cached interval of a video stream is not fixed to the prefix but is sliding over the complete stream. This is helpful if several requests for the same video stream arrive at short intervals. The first request would start the caching process and all following requests that arrive within a certain period after the first one would be served from the cache. The third caching strategy, i.e., the segment based caching, is a generalization of the former ones as it divides the multimedia streams that should be cached into segments which are defined as the smallest units that can be cached.

	Prefix Caching	Sliding Interval Caching	Segment Based Caching
Complexity	++	o	+
Efficiency	o	o	+
Flexibility	- -	-	++

Table 3.1: Suitability of different caching strategies for adaptive video streaming

For these three caching strategies we investigated their complexity, efficiency and flexibility particularly with regard to their suitability for adaptive video streaming with mobile devices. Table 3.1 shows the results for all three strategies. The prefix caching strategy is best suited in terms of their complexity as it can be implemented very easily. In sum, the segment based caching strategy could be identified as being suitable for our multimedia gateway as it provides the greatest flexibility and efficiency of these three strategies. Nevertheless, we are aware that there are a lot of further multimedia caching strategies proposed in the literature, and implementing the best strategy is out of scope of this work. Nevertheless, we implemented the ability of multimedia caching in a way that allows an easy integration of further caching strategies into our gateway, which allows a simple integration of further caching algorithms into our system.

Caching Implementation

For the caching implementation, we created two different SHs that can be integrated into the server side data path, as illustrated in figure 3.5. The `CacheSinkSH` is used to store the media stream in the cache, whereas the `CacheSourceSH` is used to read a data stream from the cache. A central class called `CacheManager` takes care of the current cache state by using a specified `CacheStrategy`. If caching is enabled, each RTP packet that is processed by the `CacheSinkSH` will be pushed to the client side data path as well as to the `CacheManager`. By using a specified `CacheStrategy`, the `CacheManager` decides whether the current packet should be cached or not. In the case that the packet should be cached, the `CacheManager` will store the data packet in the local file system.

When a client opens an RTSP session, the gateway asks its `CacheManager` whether the requested stream is stored in the cache or not. If it is stored in the cache, the gateway will stream the cached version of the stream instead of creating a new server RTSP session. If the requested stream is not cached, the gateway will create a server RTSP session and will send the stream to the client, while at the same time may store it in its cache, according to the used `CacheStrategy`.

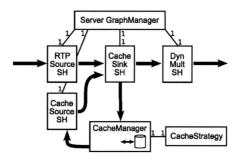

Figure 3.5: Caching implementation

Gateway Cooperation

As one of the requirements of our gateway is to support mobility of the clients in a target scenario that contains more than one gateway in the access network, it may occur that a client requests a media stream that is not cached at its current gateway but on a remote gateway in the network. In this situation it would be beneficial to stream from the remote gateway instead of streaming from the origin server. Therefore, we implemented a simple gateway cooperation mechanism that allows neighboring gateways to exchange information about their currently cached objects.

All cooperating gateways build an overlay network as illustrated in figure 3.6, and each gateway sends any changes to its cached objects to all its neighbors in the overlay network. If a gateway G1, for instance, likes to receive information about cached objects from gateway G2, it needs to register itself as a neighbor at G2. In the figure, the registration is indicated by a dashed arrow whereas the information about cached objects is illustrated by a solid arrow. After the registration, G2 sends a list of its cached objects to G1 which will be informed about any future changes at G2. To get information about other gateways, G1 may ask G2 about its other neighbors and may decide to register itself also as a neighbor at those neighbors of G2. A gateway that has at least one registered neighbor sends any changes of its cached objects to all its registered neighbors. This kind of neighbor relationship is not bidirectional and therefore, each gateway internally has two different lists: a neighbor-list containing that gateways which receive changes of its cached objects and a peer-list, containing all gateways from which it will receive information about cached objects.

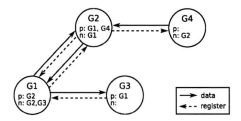

Figure 3.6: Gateway cooperation

Figure 3.6 shows an example of four cooperating gateways with their current neighbor-list (n) and peer-list (p). Gateway G1, for instance, has two registered neighbors G2 and G3 which both receive changes of cached objects at G1. Additionally, G1 has one peer G2 from which it receives information about cached objects at G2. The gateway G3 does not have any registered neighbors but receives cache changes from gateway G1, which therefore is in the peer-list of G3. Gateway G4 does not receive any information about cached object at other gateways but sends any changes to its cached objects to gateway G2.

For the implementation of the described mechanism, we defined four different messages that are exchanged between the cooperating gateways:

- A *neighbor* message registers the sending gateway as a neighbor at the receiving gateway. This message contains the IP-address as well as the RTSP-port of the sending gateway. The response to such a message only contains a positive or negative response code without any further information.

- A *cache* message informs the registered neighbors of the sender about cached objects. This message contains the IP-address and RTSP-port of the sending gateway as well as information about all currently cached objects such as names and ranges. As this message is pushed from the caching gateway to its registered neighbors like a broadcast, the response simply contains a positive response code.

- A *peer* message requests a list of all registered peers from the receiving gateway. This message does not contain further details, but the response contains IP-addresses as well as RTSP-ports of those peers registered at the gateway that received the peer message.

- A *ping* message can be used to check the existence of a gateway as well as to estimate the network delay. This message contains a timestamp that the receiver has to copy into the response message. The response can be easily extended to carry additional information about the current state of the gateway such as CPU load or the number of active sessions.

As our gateway implementation already uses RTSP for signaling, we used the two optional RTSP messages GET_PARAMETER and SET_PARAMETER to implement the cooperation mechanism. The *peer* and the *ping* messages are used to request information from a gateway whereas the other two messages are used to send information to a neighboring gateway. Therefore, we realized the *neighbor* and *cache* messages by putting the message names as well as their values into the body of a SET_PARAMETER message. The other two were realized in a similar way with a GET_PARAMETER message as illustrated in figure 3.7. Further sample request and response messages of each type of message can be found in appendix A.2.

```
SET_PARAMETER * RTSP/1.0
CSeq: 1
Content-Type: text/parameters
Content-Length: 26

neighbor: 127.0.0.1:1111
```

Figure 3.7: Example of a *neighbor* message embedded in RTSP

Within such an overlay network of cooperating gateways, each gateway is aware of all cached objects of all its peers. If a client requests a media stream that is cached on a remote gateway, the gateway that received the client's request establishes an RTSP session with the remote gateway and forwards the stream to the client. Additionally, the gateway may also decide to cache the stream locally for later use, according to its implemented caching strategies.

When streaming from a remote cache the startup delay will be slightly higher compared to streaming from the local cache. For the evaluation of this delay, we did some measurements on a small test setup consisting of one client and two gateways in a 100 Mbit/s local area network as well as a remote server on the Internet. For the Internet connection we used an ADSL connection with a downstream capacity of 6 Mbit/s. With this setup we tested three different streaming situations:

1. *Streaming from server:* In this situation the client uses a gateway and requests a video stream that is not cached.

2. *Streaming from local cache:* In this situation the client requests a video stream that is cached locally at the used gateway.

3. *Streaming from remote cache:* In this situation the client requests a video stream that is not cached at the local but at a neighboring gateway.

For each situation we evaluated the delay between the RTSP-PLAY message sent by the client and the first RTP packet received at the client. For each situation we repeated the start of the streaming session 100 times. Figure 3.8 shows the measurement results. The delay for streaming directly from the server expectedly produced the highest delay of 57.20 milliseconds on average which mainly results from the delay of the Internet connection of 36.42 milliseconds on average. Streaming from the cache at the local gateway produced the lowest delay of 13.62 milliseconds on average. In the third situation when streaming from the cache of a remote gateway, the delay increased to 24.63 milliseconds on average which results from the session setup between both gateways.

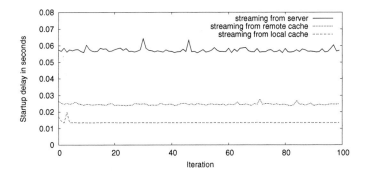

Figure 3.8: Startup delay for different caching situations

3.3.6 Client Application

As a streaming client application we used the MPlayer[4] implementation. The MPlayer is a widely used and well-known open-source media player that supports a variety of different audio and video formats. Additionally, the MPlayer does also support several network and streaming protocols, including RTSP and RTP. This streaming support is achieved by using the external library Live555[5]. This library, however, does not support the extensions described for our gateway such as the gateway discovery mechanism, the capability exchange embedded in RTSP or the session transfer. Therefore, we integrated our own extension into the MPlayer so that we were able to use all of the proposed extensions with the MPlayer.

---

[4]http://www.mplayerhq.hu
[5]http://live555.com

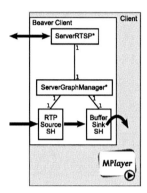

Figure 3.9: Architecture of client application

Due to the nature of an RTSP/RTP proxy, it acts as a client towards a media server and as a server towards its clients. We used that part of our gateway implementation that acts as a client to build a library that can be integrated into the MPlayer application similarly to the integration of the Live555 library. Figure 3.9 illustrates how this integration of the server side RTSP and RTP into the MPlayer is done. The MPlayer uses a very basic interface that only consists of a few functions to control the processing of the video stream. One functions is used to open the stream which results in setting up the RTSP session and sending a `PLAY` message by the integrated library. The data path of this library contains an `RTPSourceSH` and a `BufferSinkSH` that acts as a buffer for the incoming RTP packets. As the MPlayer does not support RTP, these packets are decapsulated and the payload is stored in an internal buffer. To read from this buffer the MPlayer calls a function that returns the data of a complete video frame from the buffer. When the user requests to pause or stop the playback of the stream, the MPlayer calls the corresponding function of the library that sends a `PAUSE` message to the server. By the use of the described client library, the MPlayer supports all extensions that we described in this chapter.

3.3.7 Compatibility

For our implementation we introduced several new message types or specified a different semantics for existing RTSP messages. To be able to benefit from these extensions, both parties, i.e., the gateway and the client application, need to implement a processing of the described RTSP messages. Otherwise, they would not be able to benefit from the described extensions. Nevertheless, a communication with gateways or clients that do not support the presented features is still possible, as unsupported RTSP messages should simply result in a response with a negative response code.

3.4 Summary

In this chapter we described the architecture and prototype implementation of our multimedia gateway system. The core component of this gateway is an RTSP/RTP proxy that can load different adaptation libraries at runtime and thereby provides multimedia adaptation services to the requesting clients. Additionally, the gateway may act as a flexible reflector by sharing one server session among several client sessions that consume the same media stream. This feature can be used to reduce the network load between a server and the gateway while still providing an individually adapted media stream to each requesting client. For the usability of our system we integrated a gateway discovery mechanism that is based on SLP. By using this mechanism, mobile clients may passively discover existing gateways or actively send a request for a gateway. When a client decides to use a certain gateway, it can send its profile embedded into an RTSP message to the gateway. This profile includes the capabilities of the client as well as possible user's preferences. Based on the attributes contained in the profile, the gateway can select an individually appropriate adaptation mechanism. Further features of our gateway implementation include the ability to transfer an active media session from one gateway to another as well as a cooperative caching support. The cooperative caching mechanism can be used to create a cache that is distributed over several gateways in the access network. All participating gateways build an overlay network and a client may get a stream that is cached on a remote gateway instead of establishing a new connection to the media server on the Internet.

Besides all these features, the main focus for developing our multimedia gateway was to provide a video adaptation service for mobile devices. In the following chapter, we present our multidimensional transcoding architecture as well as its implementation that can be used for video adaptation by our gateway implementation.

Chapter 4

Multidimensional Video Transcoding

The number and types of mobile devices which are capable of presenting digital video streams is increasing constantly. In most cases the devices are trade-offs between powerful all-purpose computers and small mobile devices which are ubiquitously available and range from cellular phones to notebooks. This great heterogeneity of mobile devices makes video streaming to such devices a challenging task for content providers. Each single device has its own capabilities and individual requirements, which need to be considered when sending a video stream to it. Therefore, one key aspect of our research work dealt with the design of multimedia gateway architectures that can cope with the characteristics of our target scenario such as the one sketched above. As a result of this part of our work we presented a multimedia gateway in chapter 3 which is capable of adapting video streams to the requirements of the requesting mobile client.

However, we have not yet discussed how to perform this adaptation. This chapter now focuses on this major part of our research work and discusses in detail video adaptation for mobile devices. In this context it is important to be also aware of some typical, partly also non-technical characteristics of mobile video streaming scenarios. Mobile devices, for instance, typically have smaller screen sizes, which results in lesser details visible on the screen of mobile devices compared to home entertainment displays. A user of a mobile device may watch a video stream in a variety of situations: while being at home, sitting in a park or, to name but a few, while traveling on a train. Additionally, the users of such devices may vary their viewing angel and distance more often and dynamically, compared to watching a video stream on a fixed screen. As a consequence, also the environment of mobile devices such as the audio-visual ambience as well as the network conditions, may vary more often over time compared to static devices. Thus, the experience of watching video streams on mobile devices differs to a great extent from those scenarios related to static displays usually found in the area of home entertainment. To get an idea of how different adaptation methods may affect the experience of users watching a streamed video on a mobile device, we inspect the influence of three major adaptation dimensions after describing the requirements of video adaptation for mobile devices in section 4.1. The results for adaptation in the spatial dimensions can be found in section 4.1.2 followed by the results for the temporal and the detail dimension in sections 4.1.3 and 4.1.4, respectively.

As we will see later, one of the central results of this analysis is that at least three dimensions of a video stream need to be adapted to support a great heterogeneity of devices. Therefore, we developed a processing architecture which supports the usage of different transcoding mechanisms for video adaptation in several dimensions. Based on this architecture, we implemented a multidimensional transcoder which can adapt video streams in the spatial, temporal and detail dimension. Both, our proposed architecture as well as the transcoder implementation, which were published in [7, 8], are presented in detail in section 4.2.

The analysis of the adaptation requirements indicates that the kind of adaptation which is performed on the video stream, does not solely depend on technical parameters of a video stream like bit rate, resolution or frame rate. Instead it is also necessary to identify the type of content of a video stream. In our work we use a frame-by-frame approach to content analysis. Therefore, we define different metrics which can be used to analyze the content of each video frame within the compressed domain. In the context of our research, this kind of content analysis can, for instance, be used to support the detection of scene changes. This new approach to video content analysis within the compressed domain, which was published in [9], is presented in section 4.3.

4.1 Video Adaptation for Mobile Devices

Video streaming to mobile devices is mainly restricted by the limitation of the display resolution, the processing power, the available memory size and the remaining energy of the mobile device as well as the available network bandwidth. Although mobile video devices are getting more and more powerful, the problem of limited resources will remain in the future, since quality demands are rising as well.

Table 4.1 shows the impact of different video characteristics such as the spatial resolution or the video encoding format on the resource requirements, which the decoding device has to satisfy. Starting from a video stream which can be received and decoded by a certain device without limitations, each column of this table shows a '+' if an adaptation of the given aspect of the video has an impact on the resource given in the corresponding row or a 'o' otherwise. As one can see in the first column, especially the *spatial resolution* of a stream has an impact on each limited resource. When reducing the frame size of a video stream, its bit rate is reduced as well, which in turn also reduces the necessary network bandwidth for transmission of the video. For the decoding of video streams, at least one reference frame needs to be held in memory to decode motion compensated frames. Because of smaller frame sizes, the memory consumption of the reference frames is reduced as well. Furthermore, the required processing power for decoding and therefore the energy consumed by the device are reduced as well.

A reduced number of frames, i.e., a lesser *temporal resolution* of the video, results in a lower bit rate of the stream which needs to be transmitted over the network. Additionally, a lower number of frames needs to be processed for decoding the stream. Thus,

	Spatial Resolution	Temporal Resolution	Detail Resolution	Video Format	Video Content
Display	+	o	o	o	o
Processor	+	+	+	+	o
Memory	+	o	o	+	o
Energy	+	+	+	+	+
Network	+	+	+	+	o

Table 4.1: Impact of encoding parameters

the temporal resolution of a video stream has an impact on the processing power and the energy needed for decoding the stream as well as on the network bandwidth needed for transmission. The screen size is obviously not affected, as the spatial resolution is not changed. The memory consumption usually is also not affected because reference frames still need to be hold in memory. Apart from H.264 video, the motion vectors in a video stream are interpreted as pointing to the directly preceding or succeeding frame which is no B-frame. Therefore, the number of frames, which needs to be hold in memory for decoding is usually not changed when the number of frames is reduced.

A similar impact on the resources can be found in the case of the *detail resolution*. A lower detail resolution, i.e., a lower visual quality of a video stream results in a reduced number of DCT values which needs to be transmitted over the network and to be processed by the processor. Park et al. demonstrated that the energy consumption of the video decoding process can be reduced down to 58 % by increasing the quantization level which at the same time results in a quality decrease of only 13 % [95]. An adaptation of the detail resolution, however, does not have an impact on the screen size and the memory consumption because the number of pixels of the decoded frames are not changed by this adaptation.

The video codec used for encoding a video stream may also have an impact on most resources of the decoding client. However, compared to the aforementioned aspects, an adaptation of the video format usually only has a low gain. Only in the case that a client does not support the *video format* of a stream it is useful to change the syntax of the bit stream. However, simply changing the syntax of a video stream usually does not utilize the whole potential of the target format. When, for instance, the video format should be changed from MPEG-2 to MPEG-4, the produced stream will not reach the coding efficiency as if it was directly encoded in MPEG-4. Usually the main focus of changing the video format is to enable the client to decode the video stream but not to lower the resource requirements of the client. Thus, it is not necessary to discuss the influence of different video codecs any further in the context of coping with limited resources at the client.

Besides the aforementioned aspects it may also be useful to adapt the *video content* of a stream. If a user, for instance, is not interested in the complete video stream but rather in some kind of summary of the content such an adaptation may be used. An example of such a summary could be the reduction of a soccer match to the key sequences as it can be found in the sports news on TV. As such an adaptation of the video content may result in a reduced length of the video stream, the impact of different video contents is typically confined to the remaining energy of the device.

Based on the resource limitations of mobile devices we can clearly identify four video characteristics that mainly influence whether a requesting device can consume a digital video stream or not. These are the spatial resolution, the temporal resolution, and the detail resolution of a video stream as well as the video format. The latter aspect, however, is some kind of a special case because its focus is not to fulfill any resource limitation of the device but to enable the client to decode the video stream at all. Therefore, in our work we concentrate on video adaptation of the former three resolutions. Our adaptation approach, however, is not limited to these adaptation dimensions and can be easily extended as we will see later on.

4.1.1 Adaptation Requirements

The main goal of video adaptation is to produce a video stream which fits to the requirements of the requesting client. In video streaming scenarios, a requested video stream firstly needs to be transmitted to the client over the network. If the bit rate of a video stream is higher than supported by the network connection, the receiving client will not be able to receive the stream properly. In such a situation, the bit rate at which the client can receive the stream from the network is the most limiting requirement. In the previous section we identified the impact of different video characteristics on the resource requirements at the receiving client. The bit rate of a video stream mainly depends on three different dimensions: the spatial resolution, the temporal resolution and the detail resolution of the stream. However, a certain target bit rate can be achieved by several combinations of adaptation dimensions. The temporal resolution of a video stream, for instance, might be reduced while keeping the detail quality of the remaining frames. Another possibility would be to reduce the detail quality while keeping the frame rate of the stream. Both approaches may achieve a similar bit rate reduction, and it needs to be identified which approach produces a better quality. For the spatial resolution, a similar situation exists. A video stream might be downscaled to the resolution of the receiving device or even further to retain a higher detail quality for each single frame. Altogether there are $2^3 = 8$ different combinations of the three mentioned adaptation dimensions which may achieve a lower bit rate. Additionally, for each dimension different adaptation parameters may exist. Each of these dimensions and parameters might lead to different other limitations and will be discussed in the next sections.

If the capacity of the network connection is not the limiting factor, for instance in a home entertainment scenario with a network connection that supports high bit rates between the video source and the client, the situation is much easier as the temporal and the spatial resolution of a video stream can be adapted independently. If the display resolution of the requesting client is the limiting factor, the spatial resolution of the video stream needs to be tailored accordingly. If the temporal resolution of the stream is the only or an additional limiting factor, the frame rate needs to be reduced. In both situations, the detail quality is not reduced as the available bit rate of the network connection is not the limiting factor.

4.1.2 Spatial Adaptation

Adaptation of the spatial resolution can be used to reduce the bit rate of the stream and to meet the resolution of the client display. The latter aspect can be optimally achieved by reducing the spatial resolution of the stream to exactly the display resolution of the receiving device. However, better quality results might be achieved by reducing the spatial resolution further while keeping the detail resolution at a higher level. Another possibility is to keep the spatial resolution higher than the display resolution while reducing the detail resolution of each frame. Thus, three different possibilities for the target resolution can be distinguished:

i) The target resolution is higher than the display resolution.

ii) The target resolution is exactly the same as the display resolution.

iii) The target resolution is lower than the display resolution.

Sequence Name	Motion/Details
Akiyo	very low
Mother-Daughter	low
Silent	low
Deadline	low
Container	low
Hall-Monitor	medium
Highway	medium
Foreman	medium
Coastguard	medium
Mobile	high

Table 4.2: Video sequences

To identify which target resolution produces the best quality, we encoded several well-known video sequences at different spatial resolutions and bit rates. For each encoded sequence, we evaluated the produced quality in terms of the average Y-PSNR values, as described in section 2.6, with respect to two different target resolutions: i) CIF resolution with 352×288 pixels and ii) a resolution of 264×216 pixels, which is CIF downscaled by a factor of 0.75 on both axes. Table 4.2 shows the names as well as the amount of motion for each test sequence that was used.

Each video sequence was encoded at different bit rates ranging from 40 kbit/s to 480 kbit/s with a temporal resolution of 25 frames per second and three different spatial resolutions, i.e., CIF resolution, a resolution of 264×216 pixels and QCIF resolution at 176×144 pixels. For the encoding process we used the MEncoder from the MPlayer project[1] in combination with the MPEG-4 codec from the FFmpeg project[2]. The average Y-PSNR values were calculated with respect to the target resolution. Therefore, the MPlayer was used for decoding the video frames and the PSNR values of each decoded frame were computed by the use of some tools from the Netpbm project[3]. For the target resolution of 352×288 pixels, i.e., for the CIF resolution, we calculated the PSNR values from the decoded and upscaled pictures. For the second target resolution of 264×216 pixels, we firstly downscaled the version encoded at CIF resolution to fit to 264×216 pixels, which simulates the scaling process necessary on the decoding device with the given target resolution. Afterwards, all versions were upscaled to CIF resolution again in order to calculate the PSNR values.

Figure 4.1 illustrates the processes used to create the different versions of the stream as well as the versions used to compute the PSNR values. For the target resolution of 264×216 pixels the upper path for producing the stream at CIF resolution is used whereas for the target resolution of 352×288 pixels the lower path is used.

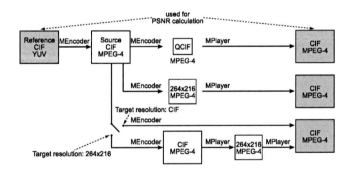

Figure 4.1: Evaluation process for different spatial target resolutions

[1] http://www.mplayerhq.hu
[2] http://www.ffmpeg.org
[3] http://netpbm.sourceforge.net

For each video sequence there exists a lower and an upper bound for the bit rate that can be achieved by the used encoder at the given spatial and temporal resolution. These bounds result from the limitation of the quantizer scale value, as presented in 2.1.1. At the lower bound the encoder uses the highest possible quantizer scale value and therefore produces the lowest possible quality. At the upper bound the encoder accordingly uses the lowest possible quantizer scale value and produces the highest possible quality. The values of these bounds depend on the characteristics of each video sequence and therefore, the following graphs do not always contain PSNR values for the full range of bit rates between 40 and 480 kbit/s.

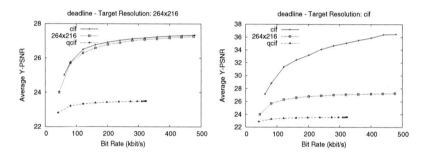

Figure 4.2: Video quality at different spatial resolutions - deadline sequence

Figure 4.2 exemplarily shows the average Y-PSNR values of the deadline sequence for each target resolution compared to the bit rate of each stream. It can be observed that in both situations a lower resolution than the target resolution results in substantial lower PSNR values for all bit rates. For the lower target resolution of 264×216 pixels, it can be further seen that encoding at a higher resolution slightly increases the produced quality. The reason for this increase is that the motion estimation in the encoder benefits from the higher resolution. However, this quality increase resulting from the higher resolution is not significant. To further evaluate the better quality of the stream encoded at a higher resolution we produced additional video streams at intermediate resolutions between 264×216 and 352×288 pixels. Figure 4.3 shows the PSNR values for these intermediate resolutions. For bit rates above 40 kbit/s it can be clearly seen that the version of the stream with the same resolution as the target resolution of 264×216 pixels produces better results compared to those versions with higher resolutions, except the original resolution of 352×288 pixels.

The results for most of the other sequences show very similar results to those of the deadline sequence. Only for some sequences we observed that the PSNR values of the version with a resolution higher than the target resolution were about 1 dB increased than the PSNR values of the version at the target resolution. As both the sequence

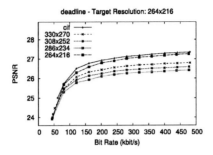

Figure 4.3: Video quality at different intermediate spatial resolutions - deadline sequence

with the lowest amount of motion and visible details as well as the sequence with the highest amount of motion and visible details showed this effect of higher PSNR values, we could not clearly identify any similarities in the affected sequences. Figure 4.4 shows the results of the mobile sequence as an example of such a sequence. Further details about this evaluation process, the tools we used and the results for all other sequences, can be found in the appendix B.1.

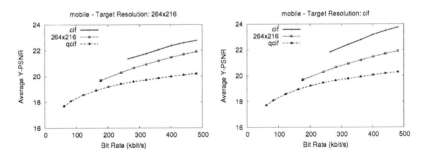

Figure 4.4: Video quality at different spatial resolutions - mobile sequence

For the deadline sequence, figure 4.2 clearly shows the aforementioned upper bound of the bit rate for the lowest spatial resolution. For QCIF resolution the highest possible quality was achieved at a bit rate of 324.29 kbit/s. Due to the high amount of motion in different directions of the mobile sequence, the graphs in figure 4.4 show the lower bound for CIF resolution at 263.86 kbit/s and at 175.02 kbit/s for a resolution of 264×216 pixels. Any further reduction of the bit rate could only be achieved by reducing the spatial resolution.

A screen resolution of 352×288 pixels is quite low and may not be representative for the great range of different devices. Therefore, we also evaluated the produced quality for a higher resolution of 704×576 pixels. This resolution is four times higher than CIF resolution and is therefore also called 4CIF. For this resolution we used two further test sequences as the previously used sequences were only available at a maximum resolution of CIF. One is called the *harbour* sequence and shows some slowly moving boats in a small harbor. Due to the great amount of moving objects in this sequence it has similar characteristics as the mobile sequence. The second sequence is called *soccer* and shows some soccer players on the playing field. From the amount of motion it is comparable to the foreman sequence. For both sequences, we evaluated the produced quality at a target resolution of 528×432 pixels which is the original resolution downscaled by a factor of 0.75. In this case it was sufficient to concentrate on only one target resolution that is lower than the original resolution of the streams because the results for the target resolution of 352x288 pixels showed very clearly that reducing the spatial resolution any further than needed for the target resolution produces bad quality results.

Figure 4.5 shows the average Y-PSNR values of both sequences for this target resolution. The results are quite similar to the previous ones: The differences between the PSNR values are quite small for the versions at the original and at the target resolution. The only difference that can be seen from the graphs is that for bit rates below approximately 2500 kbit/s the PSNR values of the video stream with the target resolution are slightly above those of the stream with the original resolution. For bit rates above this rate the video stream with the original resolution produced slightly better results. This may result from the greater range of bit rates that can be achieved for the higher resolutions. For the soccer sequences we achieved bit rates up to 14000 kbit/s and for the harbour sequence we achieved even higher rates.

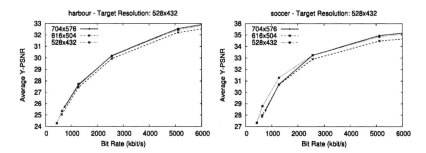

Figure 4.5: Video quality at different spatial resolutions - harbour and soccer sequence

However, as mentioned before, there are other resource limitations which need to be considered as well. When using another spatial resolution than the target resolution, more processor cycles are needed for the spatial scaling at the receiving client, which usually results in a higher energy consumption at the device. This could only be justified by a substantial quality increase. Our evaluation, however, did not show a significant increase of the produced quality in the cases where the video was encoded at a resolution different from the target resolution.

In summary, it can be observed that any reduction of the spatial resolution other than that needed to adapt a video stream to the display resolution of the receiving device is usually not sensible with respect to the quality of the stream. With respect to the bit rate of the video stream, a reduction of the resolution more than needed to meet the display resolution may be necessary in order to reduce the bit rate of the stream as needed. However, this might result in additional quality loss and further processing cycles needed for any spatial scaling process on the receiving device.

4.1.3 Temporal Adaptation

Another possibility to reduce the bit rate of a video stream in order to meet the requirements of a requesting client, is the reduction of the temporal resolution. In contrast to an adaptation of the spatial resolution, there typically is no temporal target resolution which needs to be achieved. Unless the requesting device has any frame rate limit, the only criteria which can be used to identify a reasonable frame rate is the produced quality. Therefore, we need to determine if the quality of a stream can be increased by reducing the frame rate rather than reducing the detail resolution, which usually is used to reduce the bit rate of the stream.

In the context of temporal adaptation, the analysis of PSNR values would not help to evaluate and compare the produced quality, because the PSNR values would be computed from streams at different frame rates. PSNR values are computed frame-by-frame with respect to a reference stream. If the produced stream has a frame rate lower than the reference stream, the missing frames need to be interpolated. This interpolation usually results in poor PSNR values if there is some amount of motion in the sequence. A second possibility is to compute the PSNR values for the resulting frames only. This method usually results in higher PSNR values if the frame rate is reduced. Additionally, as the PSNR values are computed on a frame-by-frame basis, the impact of a smooth motion on the produced quality is neglected. Therefore, we developed an evaluation process that involves interviews with potential users (subjective quality assessment) and is based on user-responses to different test videos. We encoded different video sequences at different frame rates and presented them on a mobile device to potential users. As the mobile device, we used a PDA[4] with a 3.5 inch display and QVGA resolution (320 × 240 pixels).

We chose four different video sequences which cover a broad range of different characteristics such as genre, the amount of motion, the number of scene cuts and regions of interest. Figure 4.6 shows example frames from each chosen sequence. The first

---

[4]Hewlett Packard iPAQ HX2750

(a) News (b) Soccer

(c) Animation Movie (d) Natural Movie

Figure 4.6: Test video sequences

sequence was taken from a news broadcast, showing a speaker in front of a static background intercepted by short news clips. This is a typical news sequence including parts with a low amount of motion alternating with passages with higher amount of motion. The second sequence is a short section from a soccer game broadcasted on TV. In the beginning of this sequence, the playing field is shown from the perspective of the audience followed by some close-ups of single players and groups of players. The characteristics of this sequence are quite different from the news sequence because there is a high amount of movement in the foreground as well as in the background. This sequence is also a good example for a small region of interest because people who are watching a soccer game usually are more interested in the movements of the ball than in the movements of the audience. The third and fourth test sequences were chosen from movie trailers available on the Internet: one sequence was taken from an animation movie and another one was taken from a movie with natural video content. Both sequences have a high number of cuts as well as a high amount of motion but differ in the genre. The length of all four sequences was between 75 and 90 seconds. Table 4.3 shows the encoding parameter used. All sequences were encoded with a fixed spatial resolution which fitted best to the screen of the mobile device used in the test situations and a constant bit rate of 180 kbit/s, which is a typical rate for videos on the Internet [96].

As the temporal resolution, we used three different frame rates: the original, 12 or 5 frames per second (fps). The original frame rates for the news and soccer sequences were 25 fps and 24 fps for the movie trailers.

Sequence	Resolution	Frame Rates	Bit Rate
News	320×240	5, 12, 25 fps	180 kbit/s
Soccer	320×240	5, 12, 25 fps	180 kbit/s
Animation Movie	320×180	5, 12, 24 fps	180 kbit/s
Natural Movie	320×180	5, 12, 24 fps	180 kbit/s

Table 4.3: Video sequences and encoding parameters

All frame rate variants of each sequence were presented to a test person in changing order to avoid any effects resulting from the order of the variants. The video sequences were displayed in full-screen mode on the mobile device that the participants held in their own hands. The environment during the tests included typical indoor and outdoor situations where people may watch videos on a mobile device. Each participant was asked to choose his or her preferred version of the video. Finally, they were also asked to rate the preferred version with a grade from 1 (best) to 6 (worst). The tests were conducted with a total number of 50 non-expert users with ages between 21 and 59 years. Each video sequence was rated by 36 to 50 of these different test persons.

Figure 4.7 shows the preferred frame rates for each test sequence. For the soccer sequence, 70.0 % of all participants preferred the version with a frame rate of 12 fps, 16.0 % preferred the version with 25 fps, 10.0 % preferred the version with only 5 fps,

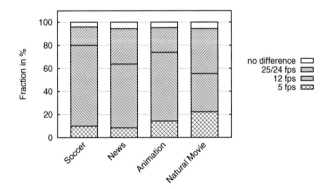

Figure 4.7: Frame rates preferred in the video tests

and 4.0 % of all participants did not notice any differences between the three different versions. For the news sequence as well as for the sequence from the animation movie, we can see very similar results. For the news sequence the version with a frame rate of 12 fps was preferred by 55.56 % of the users and for the animation sequence this version was preferred by 59.52 % of all participants. Thus, for three of the four sequences the version with the halved frame rate of 12 fps was preferred by the majority of the users. Especially in the case of the soccer sequence, a very clear preference of the version with 12 fps can be seen.

Only in the case of the natural movie trailer the test persons slightly preferred the version with the higher, i.e., the original frame rate. 38.88 % of the users preferred 25 fps and 33.33 % preferred a rate of 12 fps. Also the amount of users which preferred the version with only 5 fps is noteworthy with 22.22 %. The fact that there is no significantly preferred version of the natural movie sequence may result from the characteristics of this sequence. It has a very high number of scene cuts and fades combined with a high amount of motion. Due to this characteristics, the users might not have noticed all the details between the scene cuts and therefore may prefer the higher frame rate because of a smoother motion within the sequence.

At first glance the results observed for the first three sequences that the users preferred a lower frame rate also in the case of high amount of motion such as in the soccer sequence, seems to be a bit surprising. However, this phenomenon can be explained by the number of details visible in each single frame. If the frame rate of a video stream is reduced while at the same time the bandwidth of the stream is kept, each single frame may consume more bandwidth. If there is more bandwidth available for each frame, the quantizer scale value can be reduced and the frame will contain more visible details. Especially, in video sequences with small moving objects such as a football or the players in a soccer sequence, the visual quality of each single frame seems to be more important than a smooth playback. Similar results for sequences from soccer games as one characteristic type of video sequences were also observed by McCarthy et al. in [97]. For other genres similar findings were presented for scalable video coding by Eichhorn and Ni in [98]. Only in the case when details in a video sequence are not visible any more due to a great amount of motion or a very high number of scene cuts, more test persons prefer a higher frame rate.

The users gave their preferred video sequence a grade between 1 (best) and 6 (worst). These grades are shown in the histograms for each video in figure 4.8. For all four sequences, a dominance of a good grade around 2 can be seen. The average grades given for the preferred version of the sequences are 2.31 for the soccer sequence, 2.0 for the news sequence, 2.24 for the sequence from the animation movie, and 2.0 for the natural movie sequence. This shows that the users are satisfied with the quality of their preferred video streams. In summary it can be observed that potential users of mobile

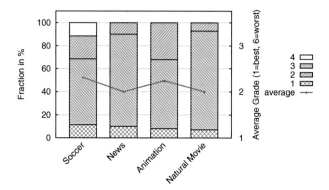

Figure 4.8: Grade of preferred video

devices prefer a higher number of details visible per frame and therefore also accept a lower frame rate of the stream. Only in the case that there are very many scene cuts within the sequence, a higher frame rate was preferred over a more detailed version to get a smoother motion between those cuts.

4.1.4 Detail Adaptation

The results from the user interviews concerning their preferred frame rate clearly indicate that a high detail resolution is a crucial factor for the users of mobile devices. The detail resolution of a video directly relates to the bit rate of the video stream which in turn is limited by the rate that the client is able to receive from the network. Thus, the detail resolution needs to be reduced as much as required from the network connection of the client.

Similar as in the discussion about the other dimensions the question arises if the detail resolution can be reduced even further while the quality is acceptable by the users of mobile devices. In order to inspect if there is a certain quality level at which users cannot notice any further quality enhancements on a mobile device, we conducted further subjective quality tests. We encoded the soccer sequence from our previous tests with a spatial resolution of 320×240 pixels and four different bit rates between 300 kbit/s and 1500 kbit/s. These different versions of the sequence were presented in pairs to potential users on the same mobile device as before. Each pair of versions was presented consecutively to the test persons in changing order. Afterwards, the test persons were asked to decide which version of the presented videos they liked more. Because the test persons may have chosen the preferred sequence randomly, they were also asked if they really noticed the better quality or just guessed.

	Version A		
	500 kbit/s	700 kbit/s	1500 kbit/s
Version B 300 kbit/s	87.80 %	85.37 %	90.24 %
500 kbit/s		70.73 %	73.17 %
700 kbit/s			60.98 %

Table 4.4: Pairwise comparison - percentages of people preferring version A over B

Four versions with different bit rates result in six pairs of videos with different bit rates. 41 non-expert users took part in these tests. Table 4.4 shows the relative frequencies of the sequences which quality was rated better in each pairwise comparison between a version A and a version B of the same video sequence. Each column in this table contains the portion of users which preferred the version with the bit rate given in the first row to the version with the bit rate given in the corresponding row. The version with a bit rate of 700 kbit/s, for instance, was chosen to have a better quality than the version with 500 kbit/s by 70.73 % of the users. Compared to the version with 1500 kbit/s, however, only 39.02 % of the users said that the quality of the 700 kbit/s version was better.

These results show that there is a clear preference for those versions of the soccer sequences with a higher bit rate and therefore also a higher detail resolution. For all six comparisons together, 78.04 % of the users chose the sequence with the higher bit rate. Table 4.5 shows the percentage of those participants who stated that they did not notice any differences between the two versions of the video and who chose one version more or less randomly. In summary, in 23.57 % of all comparisons the user randomly chose the preferred version. In 60.34 % of these cases, however, the users intuitively chose the version with a higher bit rate to have higher quality. This high percentage shows that we can assume that these choices were not truly by pure chance. Although the participants stated that they are not aware of any differences, the results show that the higher quality is still noticeable by the users. Thus, for this video sequence, there is no optimal quality level at a reasonable rate up to 1500 kbit/s.

	Version A		
	500 kbit/s	700 kbit/s	1500 kbit/s
Version B 300 kbit/s	7.32 %	9.76 %	9.76 %
500 kbit/s		34.15 %	39.02 %
700 kbit/s			41.46 %

Table 4.5: Percentages of people randomly preferred version A over B

4.1.5 Combined Adaptation

In the previous sections we have inspected the impact of different video adaptation dimensions on the requirements of the client. We have further identified three major dimensions which need to be adapted in order to support a great heterogeneity of mobile devices. Additionally, we analyzed how video adaptation in these dimensions may affect the quality of the produced video streams. In order to support a great heterogeneity of devices, however, a combined adaptation of the spatial, the temporal as well as the detail resolution is needed. To get an idea of how an adaptation of those different dimensions affects the bit rate of the stream, we re-encoded the test sequences that we had used before in section 4.1.2 in four different versions:

 i) with adaptation in the detail dimension

 ii) with adaptation in the temporal and the detail dimension

 iii) with adaptation in the spatial and the detail dimension

 iv) with adaptation in the spatial, the temporal and the detail dimension

Figure 4.9 exemplarily shows the bit rates of the akiyo sequence and the mobile sequence for all four different versions. Apart from the absolute values, there are only small differences between both graphs, although both sequences differ greatly in terms of the amount of motion. The graphs of the other test sequences show very similar results and therefore we only concentrate on these two examples with either very low or very high amount of motion, respectively.

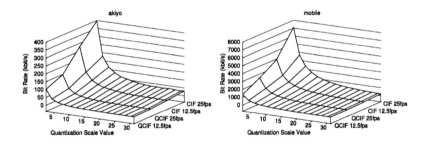

Figure 4.9: Video bit rate at different spatial, temporal and detail resolutions

The major differences in the graphs can be traced back to the amount of motion in the stream. As the akiyo sequence has a very low amount of motion, the inter-coded frames consume only a low amount of the bit rate compared to the intra-coded frames because the motion prediction produces only very small residual errors that need to be encoded. When the frame rate is reduced, the inter-coded frames need to carry much information as the differences between the frames are increasing. In case of the akiyo sequence, for instance, the size of the P-frames is increased by 41.31 % due to the frame rate reduction from 25 fps to 12.5 fps. Therefore, the bit rate of the stream is reduced just to 70.13 % although the frame rate is reduced to 50 %. The mobile sequence contains a high amount of motion and therefore, the inter-coded frames already carry a high residual error. The size of the P-frames is increased by the frame rate reduction only by 10.64 % and therefore, the bit rate of the stream is reduced to 55.35 % due to the reduction of the frame rate.

A reduction of the spatial resolution by a factor of two in both dimensions reduces the bit rate of the stream to about 36 % for both sequences in the case of the lowest quantizer scale value. Thus, here the different amount of motion does not significantly influence the amount of reduction. The reason that the bit rate is not reduced to a fourth of the original bit rate results from the motion information contained in the frames. Both graphs also show that the amount of bit rate reduction decreases for higher quantizer scale values.

In summary, we can conclude from our results for adaptation of the different single dimensions and from our results for a combined adaptation that an optimal adaptation should firstly tailor the spatial resolution of the stream to the display resolution of the requesting client. This also reduces the bit rate of the stream significantly and further reduction can be achieved by reducing the temporal resolution. Finally, the detail resolution can be reduced as needed to fine tune the bit rate of the stream to the network connection of the client.

4.2 Multidimensional Transcoding

From the analysis of different adaptation dimensions we can clearly see that an adaptation in at least three dimensions is required to support a majority of different mobile devices. One promising way for video adaptation is the use of compressed domain transcoding mechanisms, which reuse the information already contained in the video stream. However, as already presented in section 2.3, transcoding mechanisms and architectures which can be found in the literature adapt a video stream only in one or in a maximum of two dimensions, and none of the presented approaches focuses on a combined adaptation of all three dimensions. Starting from these observations and an in-depth analysis of different transcoding architectures, we developed a multidimensional transcoding approach which smartly combines one-dimensional transcoders into a transcoder chain.

In this section we firstly analyze how different transcoding mechanisms can be combined to build a multidimensional transcoder before secondly describing our approach. Afterwards, we present our processing architecture which we developed to implement a multidimensional transcoder for MPEG-4 video streams. This implementation as well as its evaluation results are presented at the end of this section.

4.2.1 Transcoding Order

When combining existing transcoding approaches, it needs to be investigated in which order the different adaptation methods should be processed. From the quality perspective, there is no implication if the temporal resolution is reduced before the spatial resolution is reduced or vice versa because both dimensions are independent of each other. A second perspective which needs to be considered is the processing time needed for the whole adaptation process. Each one-dimensional video adaptation usually reduces the amount of data of the produced stream. Thus, for a combination of different adaptation dimensions, the processing order of the transcoding steps should be chosen in a way that best reduces the amount of processed data. In the case of temporal, spatial and detail resolution reduction, the optimal processing order is quite obvious: Firstly, all frames which are not needed in the resulting video stream should be skipped. Frame skipping is rather easy in terms of processing power, and the number of frames which need to be further processed are decreased. Secondly, the resulting frames should be scaled to the designated spatial resolution. This reduces the number of DCT values of each frame. Finally, only these fewer numbers of frames with less DCT values each needs to be processed in the last transcoding step, i.e., the requantization of the remaining and downscaled frames. Thus, we will firstly reduce the temporal, then the spatial and finally the detail resolution of the stream.

4.2.2 Transcoder Decomposition

An obvious approach to combine one-dimensional transcoding approaches is to simply concatenate different transcoders to build a multidimensional transcoder. However, this would not be very beneficial in terms of processing power needed because some steps would be performed by each transcoder in the chain. For instance, at least the variable length decoding (see section 2.1.4) is needed by all transcoders to process the video stream. As most transcoders are working on dequantized values, also the inverse quantization would be processed several times by the concatenated transcoders. Thus, a more efficient way of combining the individual transcoders needs to be found.

In general, most transcoding architectures consist of three parts: one component which partially decodes the consumed video stream, a second component which modifies the values of the frames and a third component which encodes the produced video stream. Especially all those transcoders that adapt video streams in one of the three aforementioned dimensions, i.e., the spatial resolution, the temporal resolution and the detail resolution, share very similar decoding and encoding components. Therefore, by a decomposition of these components they could be used for all three transcoders and save processing power when combining such transcoders. Figure 4.10 illustrates this idea for a three-dimensional transcoder consisting of a frame skipping transcoder combined with a spatial downscaling transcoder as well as a requantization transcoder.

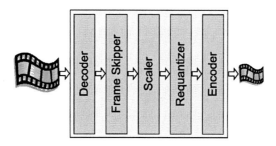

Figure 4.10: Transcoder decomposition for three transcoders

In this example the decoder component performs the bit stream parsing, the variable length decoding, the inverse quantization of the DCT values and the inverse motion compensation. The encoder correspondingly performs the motion compensation, the quantization and the variable length encoding. The variable length coding as well as the quantization processes in both directions depend on the video coding format, whereas the involved motion compensation is nearly common to several block-based video coding formats. Only in the case that the video format is changed, it may be necessary, for instance, to change the granularity of the used motion vectors. Thus, the previously mentioned decoder and encoder component of the combined transcoder, as depicted in figure 4.10, can be further decomposed. Besides the format specific encoding and decoding components additional components for the inverse motion compensation, the inverse quantization as well as for the motion compensation combined with the final quantization process are introduced. The resulting combined transcoder is illustrated in figure 4.11.

Since the motion vectors as well as the DCT values of the frames are modified by the frame skipping and scaling components, a drift-free loop is needed to reduce the transcoding error, as previously described in section 2.3. This loop computes the mo-

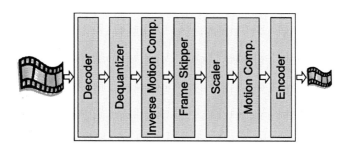

Figure 4.11: Further decomposition for combined transcoders

tion compensation as well as the quantization of the DCT values. In figure 4.11, this loop is included in the motion compensation component. As the quantization process is already included in this component, there is no need for an extra requantization component and the requantization transcoder from the previous figure can be omitted. If a requantization is required while transcoding a video stream, the motion compensation component can be configured with a newly chosen quantizer scale value.

Partial decoding, which consists of the decoder, the dequantizer and the inverse motion compensation in the figure, is necessary before skipping a frame in the transcoder. This is because the skipped frame might be referenced by other frames. Only in the case of B-frames this might not be necessary because B-frames usually are not referenced by other frames[5]. Therefore, we can further decompose the decoder component into one component which solely decodes the header information, including the frame type and a second component which performs the further decoding. Figure 4.12 shows the fully decomposed combined transcoder which is able to adapt incoming video streams in the temporal, the spatial and the detail dimension.

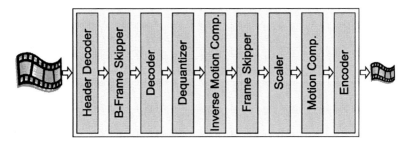

Figure 4.12: Further decomposition of the decoder for combined transcoders

4.2.3 Processing Architecture

In the previous section we have exemplarily decomposed different existing one-dimensional transcoders in order to save processing power when combining them to build up a multidimensional transcoder. Some of these decomposed transcoding components depend on the encoding format of the processed video and some do not. Thus, by exchanging the format specific component we can get a transcoder for other video formats or for heterogeneous transcoding from one format to another. Therefore, we developed a processing architecture which allows a new composition of such decomposed transcoders.

---

[5]However, some video coding standards such as AVC/H.264 [14] allow B-frames to be used as reference frames, too.

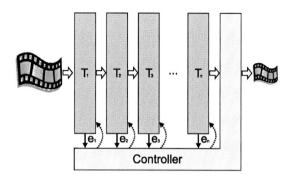

Figure 4.13: Processing architecture for transcoder modules

Figure 4.13 illustrates the core components of our architecture. It consists of several transcoding modules T_i which build a transcoder chain together with a controller. The controller is responsible for the setup and configuration of the transcoder chain. Therefore, it connects different transcoding modules T_i as needed for the video adaptation into the chain. Each transcoding module can consume and produce video frames if another module requests a frame from it. The controller acts in a similar way, i.e., it consumes frames from the transcoding modules and produces adapted frames whenever another module requests a frame from it. Thus, the transcoding chain is working passively. Whenever a frame is requested from the controller, it requests the next frame from the last transcoding module in the chain, i.e., T_n in the figure, which in turn requests and consumes a frame from its connected transcoding module and so on. The first transcoding module in the chain, i.e., T_1 in the figure, reads the original frame from one or more video sources. Examples of such sources are files, network streams or live streams from a camera. Each transcoding module adapts the processed frame as previously configured by the controller which finally writes the transcoded frame to an output stream such as a file or a network stream. The decision about how a frame is adapted is made in the controller and the transcoding modules just execute this. Therefore, we integrated a possibility for the transcoding modules to inform the controller about their current state. In compliance with the observer design pattern [99], each transcoder in the chain can generate transcoder events e_i by which the controller is notified. Therefore, each transcoding module provides a method which the controller may use to register itself as an observer. The controller, on the other hand, provides a method which the transcoding modules may use to notify the controller. A header decoding module, for instance, may inform the controller about the current type of frame as well as its coded size. The controller may react to this event by configuring a frame skipping transcoding module to skip this frame or not.

4.2.4 Frame Processing

When simply concatenating existing transcoding mechanisms in the transcoding chain, the frames which are passed from one transcoding module to another would be completely encoded frames. However, as we have seen in section 4.2.2, due to the transcoder decomposition, this is not a common situation in our architecture. Instead, the video frames passed from one transcoding module to another are typically neither completely encoded nor completely decoded. But they may be partially decoded from the bit stream at different stages. The DCT values, for instance, may have already been parsed from the bit stream but have not been dequantized yet. To indicate the actual coding state of a frame, we defined the following five states:

- *encoded*: The frame is completely encoded, as it was read from the input stream.

- *partially decoded*: The header information of the frame has been parsed from the bitstream.

- *quantized*: The entropy decoding was performed, and all parts of the frame are completely parsed and filled into local data structures for further processing.

- *dequantized*: The DCT values of the frame are dequantized.

- *IMC*: The inverse motion compensation (IMC) has been computed, and the frame does not contain temporal dependencies anymore.

Frames which are read from the input stream without any decoding are completely encoded and their encoding state is set to *encoded*. After the format specific decoding of the header information, the encoding state of the frame is changed to *partially decoded*. Further frame decoding such as variable length decoding, or inverse scanning of the quantized DCT values changes the encoding state of the frame to *quantized*. The next step of decoding is the dequantization the DCT values, which changes the state of the frame to *dequantized*. The final decoding step needed for transcoding is the computation of the inverse motion compensation after which the state of the frame is changed to *IMC*. Figure 4.14 shows the state chart of the different frame states.

However, not all frames have to traverse all different frame states. For instance, in the case of frame dropping, B-frames may be dropped already in the *partially decoded* state and then will not be processed any further. Another example is the case that only a requantization of the stream shall be performed. Then, the computation of the IMC can be omitted, and no frame will get into the *IMC* state.

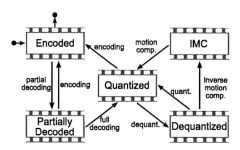

Figure 4.14: Frame states

Frame Data Structure

For the communication between different transcoding modules in the chain we have created a data structure to hold all pieces of information that belong to a frame. This data structure also contains the raw data of the encoded frame as it was read from the bit stream. In every step where further data is decoded, the according parts of the structure are filled with decoded information. After decoding of the header information, for instance, the frame type is stored in the data structure, and the encoding state of the frame is changed.

The frame data structure is defined by several interfaces as illustrated in figure 4.15. The main interface is the `Frame` interface by which the entire information of a frame is accessible. The macro blocks of a frame are accessible by the `MacroBlock` interface, and each macro block contains several blocks and motion vectors which are accessible by their corresponding interface. The `StreamInfo` interface is used to access information about the whole stream which does not belong to any single frame. An example of such information is the video object layer (VOL) in MPEG-4 video. Each frame object should contain all necessary stream information so that the entire frame can be processed without any additional information. As the frame is decoded step-by-step by different modules, it also contains the encoded bit stream of the frame which is accessible via the `BufferList` interface. This interface gives access to a list of buffers which each should contain logical segments of the stream. In the case of MPEG video, for instance, the MPEG start codes could be used for stream segmentation.

This data structure can be used to hold the entire information of a frame for all block-based video encoding formats. For each supported encoding format, a specialized implementation of the `Frame` interface is needed. By the use of this general data structure for the communication between different transcoding modules, it is possible to intermix format dependent with format independent transcoding modules in the same transcoding chain. Format independent modules like a frame skipping module do not necessarily need the information about the encoding format and can access the video frame by the use of the `Frame` interface.

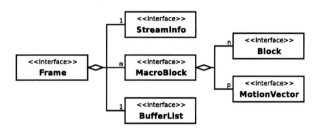

Figure 4.15: Frame interface

Frame I/O

For the exchange of video frames between different modules we defined one interface for frame production and one for frame consumption respectively (see figure 4.16). The interface `FrameSource` defines methods for frame consumption from the modules implementing this interface. The interface `FrameTarget` needs to be implemented by all modules which consume `Frame` objects from at least one `FrameSource`. Such a frame target provides several methods for adding or removing a `FrameSource` to or from it. Both interfaces also define methods that return the produced or required coding status of a produced or consumed frame respectively. Thus, when connecting a `FrameSource` to a `FrameTarget` it can be checked if the source produces frames with a correct encoding state. This information is required by the target for further processing. Therefore, each module implementing the `FrameTarget` interface defines the state of the frames it can consume as its input (ifs_i), and each module implementing the `FrameSource` interface defines the state of the frames it produces as its output (ofs_i). If two or more such modules are connected, the output frame state of each module has to match to the input frame state of its successor, i.e., $ofs_i = ifs_{i+1}$.

Transcoding Modules

As each transcoding module may consume and produce video frames in the form of a `Frame` object, the `Transcoder` interface is a generalization from the both aforementioned interfaces `FrameSource` and `FrameTarget` as illustrated in figure 4.16.

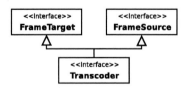

Figure 4.16: Transcoder interface

Each transcoding module may inform other objects such as the controller mentioned in the processing architecture by generating transcoder events. Therefore, we used the observer design pattern [99] with the transcoder as a subject which may inform objects of classes that implement the `TranscoderListener` interface by invoking their method `notify()`. Each object which would like to observe a transcoder module needs to register at the module which should be observed.

4.2.5 Multidimensional MPEG-4 Transcoding

Based on the proposed processing architecture we implemented a multidimensional transcoder that uses the transcoder decomposition presented in section 4.2.2. This transcoder implementation accepts video streams which are encoded in MPEG-4 advanced simple profile (ASP) and it can adapt them in the spatial, the temporal as well as in the detail dimension. The produced video stream is encoded in MPEG-4 simple profile.

In our work we created our own library for bit stream parsing and decoding of MPEG-4 ASP video streams, which provides those capabilities needed for transcoding. In contrast to existing libraries, the focus of our implementation is not on a complete decoding of all video frames but on partial decoding of each frame as needed by the transcoder modules. For the video adaptation itself, we implemented transcoding modules for the spatial, temporal and detail dimension. The frame-skipping module as well as the scaling transcoder module are implemented in a way that they are independent of the video format which they process. Thus, their usage is not limited to MPEG-4 video, but they can also be used for other block-based video coding formats such as MPEG-1/2 or H.261/3/4. To support such video formats, our implementation can easily be extended by simply adding new decoder and encoder modules which are capable of parsing the entire video streams. Thus, to extend our implementation to a heterogeneous transcoder, where input and output encoding differ, only one end of the transcoder chain needs to be changed.

In the following sections we give detailed information about the different transcoding modules of our multidimensional MPEG-4 transcoder. Firstly we discuss different options for the frame skipping module. Secondly, we present information about the implemented spatial downscaling module. Afterwards, we describe the available options for the quantization module. Finally, we present the whole transcoder chain as developed for multidimensional MPEG-4 transcoding.

Frame Skipping

If frames of a video stream are to be skipped, it needs to be distinguished whether the skipped frame is used as a reference frame by other frames or not. For video streams encoded as MPEG-1/2/4 or H.261/3 video, the latter case exists whenever a B-frame should be skipped. Thus, the B-frame skipping module is very simple as it just discards

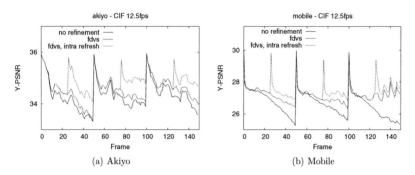

Figure 4.17: Quality of different motion vector refinement methods for frame skipping

the B-frame whenever the controller requests to skip the next frame. The P-frame skipping module similarly skips a frame whenever the controller requests this. As P-frames are usually referenced by other frames, all motion vectors of those referencing frames would get invalid after discarding the current P-frame. The simplest way to solve this problem is to interpret those invalid motion vectors as to point to the previous not skipped frame. However, this reinterpretation introduces a transcoding error, which can be reduced by using some motion vector refinement method. Our implementation of the P-frame skipping module uses the forward dominant vector selection (fdvs) as described in section 2.4.3. Due to the nature of motion compensation, the introduced transcoding error will propagate until the next I-frame. Therefore, we also implemented the possibility to insert additional I-frames into the stream, by simply changing the frame type from a P- to an I-frame. In the literature, this idea of introducing additional intra-coded frames or macro blocks is called intra-refresh approach [50, 35]. The disadvantage of the intra-refresh method is that intra-coded frames consume a higher number of bits compared to P-frames. To reduce the amount of additionally introduced bits, we increase the quantizer scale value for those intra-refresh frames.

To illustrate the effect of different motion vector refinement methods, figure 4.17 exemplarily shows the average Y-PSNR values of two transcoded test sequences, i.e., akiyo and mobile. Both sequences were transcoded to a reduced temporal resolution, the same spatial resolution as the input stream and a fixed quantizer scale value of 10. The PSNR values were computed as described in section 2.6, by using only those frames that exist in the transcoded sequence as well as in the reference sequence. The peak values, which are common to all graphs, result from the I-frames at the frame numbers 0, 50, and 100. This nicely illustrates the effect of the aforementioned transcoding error which propagates until the next key frame. The intermediate peak values of the intra-refresh graph result from the additionally inserted intra-coded frames, which stop the propagation of the transcoding error. In can be further seen that the forward dominant vector selection increases the PSNR values. Therefore, also the visual quality of all frames increases, excluding the key frames because these are intra-coded without motion information. However, the amount of improvement depends on the amount of motion in the video sequence. The akiyo sequence contains only a very low amount of motion and therefore, the quality improvement compared to no refinement is quite low. The sequence called mobile, on the other hand, contains a high amount of motion which results in a higher quality improvement as shown in figure 4.17(b).

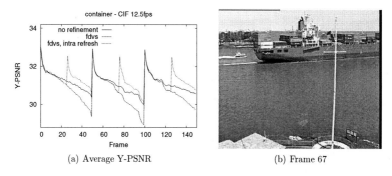

(a) Average Y-PSNR   (b) Frame 67

Figure 4.18: Container sequences with different motion vector refinement methods

The PSNR values for other video sequences show very similar results. Only in the case of the container sequence, the fdvs produces lower PSNR values. Figure 4.18(a) shows the results for the container sequence. In contrast to the graphs in figure 4.17, the PSNR values decrease faster when using the fdvs compared to the values without refinement. The container sequence shows a container ship moving slowly from left to right in the upper part of the frames. Figure exemplarily 4.18(b) shows frame number 67 of the sequence. There is a low amount of motion in this sequence and the majority of the frame shows water. The noisy structure of the water is the reason for the effect which can be observed in the PSNR values. However, from the graphs of the container sequence, it can be observed that the positive effect of the intra-refresh approach still exists for this sequence.

Besides increasing the quality, the forward dominant vector selection also reduces the bit rate of the stream. Table 4.6 shows the bit rates of the aforementioned test sequences with different refinement methods. For instance, in case of the mobile sequence, the bit rate is reduced from 1576.90 kbit/s to 901.68 kbit/s, which is a reduction of 42.82 %. The reason for this significant decrease is the reduction of the residual error encoded for each inter-coded macro block. As intra-coded macro blocks consume more bits, the intra-refresh approach increases the bit rate of the stream. In the case of the mobile sequence, the bit rate is increased to 925.48 kbit/s which is an increase of just 2.57 %, and the rate is still lower than without refinement. In the case of the container and the akiyo sequences, this bit rate reduction can be observed as well but not to that extent.

		Bit Rate (kbit/s)		
		no refinement	fdvs	fdvs + intra refresh
Sequence	Akiyo	63.31	50.59	59.28
	Container	153.54	140.12	152.42
	Mobile	1576.90	901.68	925.48

Table 4.6: Bit rates for different motion vector refinement methods

Video streams typically have a constant frame rate, and most video players rely on this. If some video frames are skipped from a stream, its frame rate is changed. In the case that the frame skipping is performed at a fixed frequency, for instance by skipping every second frame, the receiving client could be informed about the change of the frame rate. However, if frame skipping is performed more dynamically, for instance according to the movement within the stream, the decoding client may get problems decoding the stream due to the varying frame rate. In the case of MPEG-4 video such problems can be avoided by encoding each skipped frame with a special type of frame. This so called N-VOP is a frame which is not coded in the stream. Instead, only the type of frame and some timing information are encoded. According to the MPEG-4 standard [1], each N-VOP consumes only between 39 and 54 bits of the stream. During the decoding process, N-VOPs are decoded as inter-coded frames with zero length motion vectors. To be able to benefit from this feature or MPEG-4 video, we implemented all frame skipping modules in a way that they only mark the corresponding frames as not to be coded. Depending on the encoder module at the end of the transcoder chain, such frames can be encoded as N-VOPs or finally skipped. If the encoder supports the concept of N-VOPs, the receiving client is still getting a stream with a constant frame rate although some of the frames are skipped, and all problems concerning a varying frame rate are avoided.

Spatial Downscaling

The spatial downscaling module of our implementation uses a simple bilinear interpolation in the frequency domain as presented in section 2.4. This module is able to reduce the spatial resolution by a factor of two in each direction (horizontal and vertical). Thus, one downscaled macro block has to be computed from four incoming macro blocks, as illustrated in figure 4.19. In the case of I-frames, all incoming macro blocks have the same type as all of them are intra-coded. Therefore, also the newly computed macro block is intra-coded. In the case of P- or B-frames, the incoming macro blocks may have different types as MPEG-4 video also allows intra-coded macro blocks within motion compensated frames. If not all four neighboring macro blocks of such a frame have the same type, a type for the downscaled macro block has to be chosen.

Our implementation follows the mode decision approach proposed by Lee et al. [57], which can be described as follows:

- If at least one incoming MB is intra-coded, the resulting MB will also be intra-coded.

- If all incoming MBs are inter-coded, the resulting MB will also be inter-coded.

- If at least one incoming MB is not coded and all other MBs are inter-coded, the resulting MB will be inter-coded, too.

- If all incoming MBs are not coded, the resulting MB will also be not coded.

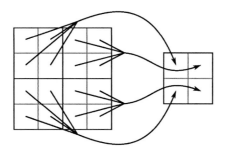

Figure 4.19: Spatial downscaling by a factor of two

If frames are motion compensated, not only their DCT values, but also their motion vectors have to be downscaled. In the case of downscaling by a factor of two, only one resulting motion vector has to be computed from four incoming vectors. Lee et al. [57] proposed to use an activity-weighted median filtering (awmf) scheme to select one of the incoming motion vectors as already described in section 2.4.4. As MPEG-4 video supports four motion vectors per macro block, the four incoming vectors can also directly be used in the downscaled macro block, each downscaled by a factor of two. However, this is only possible if each incoming macro block has exactly one motion vector. Otherwise, if at least one of the incoming macro blocks already contains four motion vectors, the activity-weighted median of the four incoming vectors can be used to select one motion vector per block.

Figure 4.20 exemplarily shows the average Y-PSNR values of four different test sequences. All sequences were transcoded from CIF to QCIF resolution with a quantizer scale value of 10 without changing their temporal resolution. The graphs denoted by *awmf* show the results if the activity-weighted median filtering scheme is used to select the resulting motion vector. The graphs denoted by *inter4v* show the results if the ability of MPEG-4 video to support four vectors per macro block is exploited. The peak values at the frames 0, 100, and 200, again, result from the I-frames in these

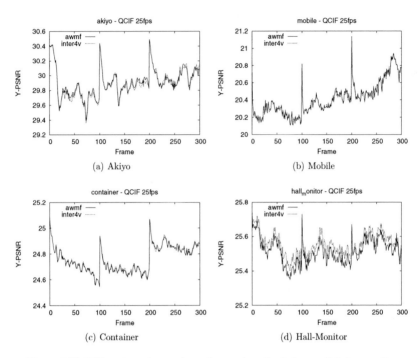

(a) Akiyo (b) Mobile

(c) Container (d) Hall-Monitor

Figure 4.20: Different morion vector refinement methods for spatial downscaling

positions. The differences of the PSNR values are very small for all test sequences and there is no clear advantage of one refinement method. For some sequences such as the hall-monitor sequence (4.20(d)) we observed that the *inter4v* variant produced slightly better results than the *awmf* variant. However, the PSNR differences are below 0.1 dB for all sequences and therefore not significant. Encoding four motions vectors per macro block instead of only consumes more bits and may lead to a smaller residual error. This again may result in a smaller bit rate. Table 4.7 shows the bit rates and average Y-PSNR values for our test sequences. For six out of the ten test sequences we got a small bit rate reduction in the *inter4v* case. Additionally, the computation of the *awmf* variant is slightly slower because of the computation of the weighted median, which is not needed for the *inter4v* variant. Thus, the *inter4v* variant should be used if possible and the *awmf* variant otherwise.

Sequence Name	awmf		inter4v	
	Bit Rate (kbit/s)	Avg. Y-PSNR	Bit Rate (kbit/s)	Avg. Y-PSNR
Akiyo	26.92	29.91	26.46	29.90
Mother-Daughter	40.88	30.01	44.24	30.05
Silent	67.83	26.86	62.70	26.90
Deadline	63.80	22.81	61.78	22.82
Container	55.63	24.76	56.62	24.76
Hall-Monitor	52.69	25.52	54.11	25.56
Highway	70.46	29.72	82.58	29.76
Foreman	149.58	26.29	144.90	26.73
Coastguard	187.63	24.41	164.84	24.44
Mobile	603.22	20.41	601.97	20.41

Table 4.7: Bit rates for different motion vector refinement methods

Quantization

The third adaptation dimension addressed by our implementation is the detail resolution, which is controlled by the quantizer scale value. As already mentioned in the section about transcoder decomposition (4.2.2), the motion compensation module (MC) already performs the quantization of the stream and therefore, no separate quantization module is needed. The MC module computes the motion compensation by using the existing and possibly redefined motion vectors. Therefore, it also performs the quantization as well as the inverse quantization of the DCT values. The MC module may use the original or a new quantization scale value, or it may also multiply the original quantization scale value by a given factor, depending on the request of the controller. However, the motion compensation as well as the inverse motion compensation are only needed if in addition to the detail resolution at least also one of the temporal or the spatial resolution are be adapted by the transcoder as well. If solely the detail resolution is adapted, the motion compensation modules are not needed. For this case we also implemented a pure requantization module, which may change the quantizer scale value as requested by the controller. As such a requantization without motion compensation, which is also called an open-loop transcoder, introduces large drift errors, we also integrated a drift error loop (see section 2.4.2) into the requantization module to build a so-called closed-loop transcoder.

Figure 4.21 shows the PSNR values for the akiyo and mobile sequences. Both sequences were transcoded with a new quantizer scale value of 10, with the open-loop as well as with the closed-loop transcoder. The graphs show very nicely the effect of the

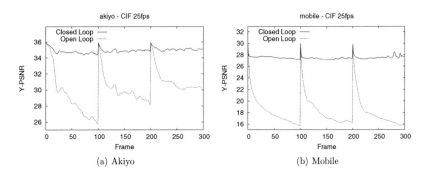

(a) Akiyo (b) Mobile

Figure 4.21: Open-loop vs. closed-loop requantization for different test sequences

introduced drift error of the open-loop approach. Starting with an I-frame the PSNR values are decreasing by about 10 dB until the next I-frame, where the drift error is reset. With the closed-loop transcoder the drift error is compensated by the drift error loop which updates the encoded residual error for each block. This results in the non-decreasing PSNR values shown in the graphs.

The visual effect of the drift error can be seen in figure 4.22 which shows the frame number 50 of the akiyo sequence produced by the open-loop and the closed-loop transcoder. A heavy distortion of the face can be seen for the open-loop variant in figure 4.22(a) which is not visible for the closed-loop variant in figure 4.22(b). Unfortunately, the compensation of the drift error increases the bit rate of the stream. For some sequences, the bit rate of the stream that was produced by the closed-loop transcoder, was two times

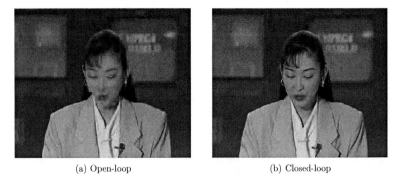

(a) Open-loop (b) Closed-loop

Figure 4.22: Frame number 50 of the akiyo sequence with and without drift-error

higher than the bit rate of the stream produced by the open-loop-transcoder. However, due to the insufficient visual quality produced by the open-loop transcoder, we decided to use a closed-loop transcoder for the multidimensional MPEG-4 transcoder.

Transcoder Chain

The complete transcoder chain of our MPEG-4 transcoder implementation is illustrated in figure 4.23. At the beginning, i.e., the left end of the chain, the *PartialDecoder* reads the video stream from the input and creates the data structure for the stream information as well as for each frame. Besides the stream information which corresponds to the whole stream, at this step only the type of frame is decoded and stored in the data structure. Afterwards, the *PartialDecoder* notifies the *Controller* by using the TranscoderListener interface before the frame is passed to the following transcoding module. The *BFrameSkipper* is placed right behind the *PartialDecoder* and reads the information about the type of each frame. If the controller requests to skip the next frame, the *BFrameSkipper* will skip the next B-frame. All other frames are simply pushed to the next transcoder module. Afterwards, the *FullDecoder* is used to decode the quantized DCT values as well as the motion vectors (in the case of intra-coded frames) of each frame. The next transcoding module is the *Dequantizer*, which computes the inverse quantization of the DCT values and the *IMC* module is used to compute the inverse motion compensation. After traversing the *IMC* module, a video frame contains all macro blocks in the frequency domain without any temporal dependencies. The *PFrameSkipper* can now skip those P-frames which the *Controller* requests to be skipped, and the *HalfScaler* can reduce the spatial resolution of the resulting frames. The *MC* component computes the motion compensation and therefore also implements the drift error loop to reduce drift errors. After the motion compensation has been computed, the frames are encoded into the output video stream by the *Encoder*.

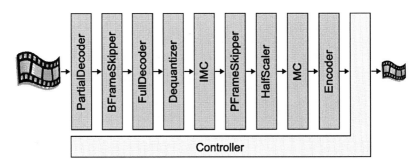

Figure 4.23: Transcoder chain for adaptation in three dimensions

If neither the temporal nor the spatial resolution needs to be adapted, a shorter transcoder chain can be used as illustrated in figure 4.24. This chain is used for adaptation of the detail resolution only and does not contain the frame skipping and downscaling modules. Additionally also the *IMC* module is missing in this chain because there is no need to compute the inverse motion compensation for a pure requantization. This example shows the advantages of our modular processing architecture, which provides the ability to realize many different transcoders by reusing existing and adding new transcoding modules.

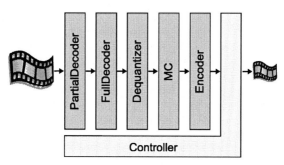

Figure 4.24: Transcoder chain for requantization

Gateway Integration

To be able to use the transcoder implementation described above for an adaptation of MPEG-4 video streams for mobile clients, we integrated the MPEG-4 transcoder into our multimedia gateway implementation presented in section 3.3. We implemented a `SubGraphSH` which contains the described multidimensional MPEG-4 transcoder. This module can be loaded by the proxy whenever a requesting client needs an adapted version of the requested video stream. Based on the profile of the client the transcoder is configured to adapt the video stream as required. Internally, incoming data packets are stored into a buffer queue from which the transcoder can read the video stream. Each transcoded frame is encapsulated into RTP packets again and afterwards pushed to the following stream handler.

Extensibility

Our current implementation of a multidimensional MPEG-4 transcoder is a prototype implementation that shows the usability of our approach. Due to the modular nature of its processing architecture, this transcoder implementation provides a great extensibility. To build, for instance, a heterogeneous transcoder that is able to transcode an incoming MPEG-2 video stream into an MPEG-4 video stream, only two modules need to be added: a *PartialDecoder* that decodes the type of each incoming frame and a *FullDe-coder* that is able to parse the incoming bit stream to fill the frame data structure, as described in 4.2.4. All other transcoder modules, which were implemented for MPEG-4 as described before, can be used as they are implemented format-independently.

4.2.6 Evaluation

For the evaluation of our multidimensional transcoder implementation we used several well-known video test sequences. These test sequences range from the akiyo sequence with very low amount of movement and spatial details to the mobile sequence with high amount of motion and spatial details. The akiyo sequence shows a woman presenting some news in front of a static background, as shown in figure 4.22. The motion in this sequence is limited to the woman's face. The mobile sequence shows a moving toy train and some other moving objects in front of a wallpaper with high spatial details. Additionally the camera slightly moves from right to left.

All test sequences were encoded to MPEG-4 by the use of the MPEG-4 codec of the FFmpeg project[6] and a fixed quantizer scale value of two so that they have the highest possible quality. All sequences have 300 frames in CIF (352 × 288) resolution, a group of video object panes (GOV) length of 100 frames and a frame rate of 25 fps. Table 4.8 shows the names, the bit rates, the average PSNR values for the chrominance as well as the amount of movement and spatial details of the video sequences used for evaluation. The given bit rates and PSNR values correspond to the encoded version of the sequences which were used as source videos in the evaluation process.

Sequence Name	Bit Rate (kbit/s)	Average Y-PSNR	Motion/Details
Akiyo	480.57	43.40	very low
Mother-Daughter	791.59	42.74	low
Silent	1182.28	41.34	low
Deadline	1291.38	41.49	low
Container	1434.72	41.19	low
Hall-Monitor	2174.87	41.24	medium
Highway	2432.76	41.51	medium
Foreman	2717.25	40.69	medium
Coastguard	3874.19	40.15	medium
Mobile	7860.63	39.86	high

Table 4.8: Characteristics of the video test sequences used for evaluation

---

[6]http://www.ffmpeg.org

Produced Quality

For the evaluation of the produced quality of the presented multidimensional transcoder we transcoded all test sequences with different transcoding parameters. Each sequence was transcoded to four different versions using the full range of possible quantizer scale values:

i) one version with the same spatial and temporal resolution as the source sequence,

ii) one version with a reduced temporal resolution,

iii) one version with a reduced spatial resolution, and

iv) one version with both, a reduced spatial and a reduced temporal resolution.

The same versions of the test sequences were also recoded with the same parameters. Therefore, the source sequences were encoded by the use of the MEncoder from the MPlayer-project[7] with the MPEG-4 codec from the FFmpeg project. To evaluate and compare the produced quality we computed the average PSNR values for the adapted video streams by using the MPlayer for decoding the video frames and computing the PSNR values of each decoded frame by using tools from the Netpbm project[8].

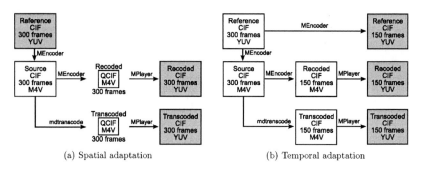

(a) Spatial adaptation   (b) Temporal adaptation

Figure 4.25: Evaluation process for spatial and temporal adaptation

Figure 4.25 illustrates the evaluation process for the adaptation of the spatial and the temporal resolution respectively. The shaded blocks in this figure indicate the frames that are used for the computation of the PSNR values. The input of the evaluation process are the uncompressed reference streams. By using the MEncoder the source streams are generated that are used as the input for the recoding and transcoding process. As mentioned before, for the recoding process the MEncoder is used. For the transcoding process, our implementation is used, which is indicated in the figure by the

---

[7]http://www.mplayerhq.hu
[8]http://netpbm.sourceforge.net

name of our binary: *mdtranscode*. For the computation of the PSNR values, the video frames needs to be decompressed from the stream. This is done by the MPlayer. If the spatial resolution of the input stream was reduced, the video frames are upscaled to the same resolution as the reference video streams as indicated in figure 4.25(a). If the temporal resolution of the input stream was reduced, only those frames are used for the PSNR calculation that are contained in both the reference and the adapted video stream. Therefore, the temporal resolution of the reference stream is reduced as well, as indicated in figure 4.25(b).

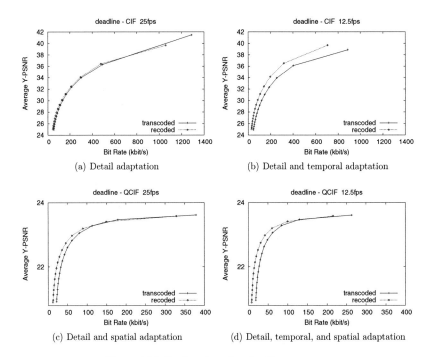

(a) Detail adaptation

(b) Detail and temporal adaptation

(c) Detail and spatial adaptation

(d) Detail, temporal, and spatial adaptation

Figure 4.26: Produced quality deadline sequence

Figure 4.26 shows the PSNR values of the deadline sequence for all four different versions i) to iv), compared to the bit rate of the produced video stream. It can be seen that the produced quality of the transcoded stream is quite close to the quality of the recoded stream for all four versions. The smallest difference in quality was achieved for the version which was adapted solely in the detail resolution, as it can be seen in figure 4.26(a). The biggest difference in quality occurred in the case that the temporal resolution was reduced while the spatial resolution was maintained as shown in figure 4.26(b). For the other two versions, when the spatial resolution was also adapted, the quality of the transcoded stream is also similar to the quality of the recoded stream. For higher bit rates the quality produced by the transcoder is also higher than the quality of the recoded versions. However, the differences are very small and therefore negligible.

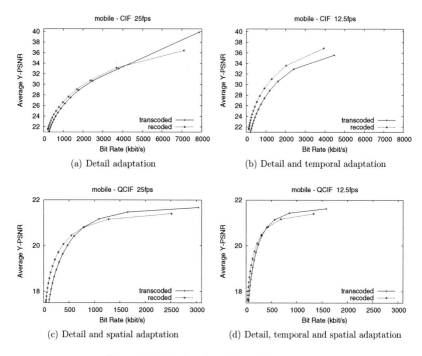

(a) Detail adaptation

(b) Detail and temporal adaptation

(c) Detail and spatial adaptation

(d) Detail, temporal and spatial adaptation

Figure 4.27: Produced quality mobile sequence

Figure 4.27 shows the results of the mobile sequence which has the highest amount of motion and also the highest bit rate of our test sequences. Similar to the results for the deadline sequence, it can be seen that the produced quality of the transcoded streams is comparable to that of the recoded sequences. Apart from the absolute values of the bit rate and the PSNR values, the shape of the graphs are very similar to those of the deadline sequence. Only the differences for higher bit rates are slightly higher than for the deadline sequence. However, these differences are still below 0.5 dB and hence still negligible.

The results for all other test sequences are very similar to those already presented here and can be found in the appendix B.2. In summary, the evaluation of the produced quality shows that the visual quality produced by our transcoder implementation is comparable to the quality which can be achieved by using a cascaded decoder and encoder.

For some parameters the quality is even higher which results from the reuse of motion information already contained in the source stream. These results also correspond to several results which can be found in the literature, e.g. in [42, 43, 50, 56].

Runtime Performance

Besides the produced quality, we also evaluated the runtime performance of our implementation. All measurements were performed on a machine with a Pentium 4 processor with 3.2 GHz and 1 GB of memory. Although the used machine has a dual core processor, only one core was used by the transcoding process, as the implementation is completely singe-threaded. For measuring the runtime we used the `gettimeofday()` function to get the current time of the system. During our measurements the machine was in single user mode without any other running processes that could interfere the measurement results. Each video sequence was transcoded at six different quantizer scale values ranging from 2 to 31 and each measurement was computed three times. From these three measurements we computed the average runtime for each quantizer scale value. From these values per quantizer scale value we computed the overall average runtime for each test sequence.

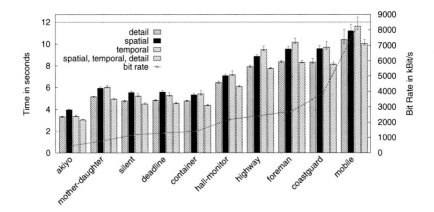

Figure 4.28: Runtime performance in total

Figure 4.28 shows the average total runtime needed for transcoding each test sequence to the aforementioned four different versions with different quantizer scale values. The error bars for each version indicate the minimum and maximum runtime. The maximum was measured with a quantizer scale value of 2 and the minimum with a value of 31. The horizontal line at y=12 in the diagram indicates the duration of 12 seconds of our video sequences. All cases where the transcoding runtime is below this line were transcoded in real-time or even faster. Only the mobile sequence could not always be transcoded in real-time by our implementation. In the case that only the temporal resolution was adapted, the runtime was slightly higher than 12 seconds for quantizer scale values lower than 5. In the three other cases the runtime was below 12 seconds for all quantizer scale values. Thus, apart from tailoring the temporal resolution and using a quantizer scale value below 5, our current prototype implementation is able to transcode all ten test sequences in real-time. Figure 4.28 additionally shows the average bit rate of the source video stream for each sequence (see also table 4.8). This nicely illustrates the correlation between the runtime of the transcoding process and the bit rate of the video sequence, which in turn usually correlates with the amount of motion and details in the sequence.

Another interesting effect that can be seen from the diagram is that for all test sequences, the adaptation of all three dimensions has the lowest runtime. The reason for this effect is the reduction of the data that needs to be processed by the following transcoding modules. Behind the frame skipping module in the transcoder chain, the spatial scaling module only needs to process half as many frames as if no frames were skipped. A similar situation exists for the motion compensation module that gets the frames from the spatial scaling module. In the case that temporal and spatial scaling with a scaling factor of two is used, the motion compensation module only needs to process half as many frames with only one fourth of the original number of DCT values.

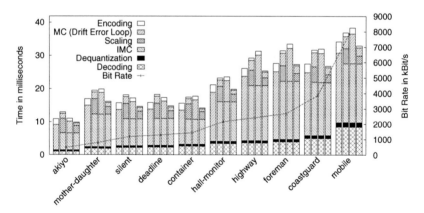

Figure 4.29: Runtime performance per transcoding module

In addition to the total runtime of the transcoding process, we also measured the runtime of each single transcoding module. Figure 4.29 shows the average runtime per frame subdivided into the average runtime per transcoding module. The first bar of each video sequence shows the time in milliseconds per frame for the case that only the detail resolution is adapted. The second bar shows the time values for the case of spatial and detail resolution adaptation, the third bar shows the values for the case of temporal and detail resolution reduction and the fourth bar shows the values for adaptation of all three dimensions. The different shadings within each bar indicate the amount of time needed to process the corresponding transcoding step. One might notice that the amount of time used for the temporal resolution adaptation is missing in these graphs. The reason for this is that the time needed for frame skipping was too short to be visible in the graphs. This amount of time was very similar for all test sequences and for the akiyo sequence, for instance, it was ten times shorter than the time needed for dequantization. Similar to the previous diagram showing the overall runtime we also included the bit rates of the sequences in this diagram. In the figure we can nicely see the correlation between the bit rate of the stream and the time needed for decoding, dequantization, IMC, MC and encoding. The amount of time needed for scaling the frames is nearly constant for all sequences as it is independent from the amount of motion or the bit rate of the stream.

The largest amount of time is used for the inverse motion compensation, which is performed in the IMC module. In the case of only adapting the detail dimension, there is no need for computing the inverse motion compensation, but the drift error loop of the MC module consumes the largest amount of time.

Although nearly all test sequences were transcoded in real time by our implementation, the overall runtime of our transcoder implementation is still very high. Compared to the runtime of the tools that were used for recoding the test sequences, our transcoder implementation needed on average between 8 and 15 times longer for adapting the test sequences. The main reason for these considerable high differences in the runtime is that we implemented our transcoder from scratch without optimized code. For the sequences with medium or high amount of motion, for instance, the time needed by our implementation to decode and dequantize the video frames was higher than the time needed by the MEncoder for the whole recoding process.

4.2.7 Discussion

In this section we presented a novel and flexible processing architecture for multidimensional video transcoding. Based on this architecture, we developed an MPEG-4 video transcoder which adapts an incoming video stream within the spatial, the temporal and the detail dimension. The evaluation of this transcoder shows good results in terms of produced quality. The runtime needed for transcoding the test sequences is, nevertheless, still quite high. However, our implementation is currently not optimized and uses quite simple transcoding methods. Patil et al. [41], for instance, showed that the time needed to compute the DCT-MC as proposed by Chang and Messerschmitt [37] that we used in our implementation could be reduced by 75 %. The time needed for spatial downscaling could also be reduced significantly by using a faster method than the bilinear interpolation, for instance that proposed by Mukherjee and Mitra [55]. Further savings could be achieved by optimizing the decoding and encoding parts of our implementation.

4.3 Content Analysis

In the first section of this chapter (4.1) we have seen that the adaptation method that produces the best quality may depend on the content of the video stream. Thus, to be able to choose optimal adaptation parameters, the content of the requested video stream needs to be analyzed, too. As the transcoder is working in the compressed domain, any content analysis needs to be done in the compressed domain, too. Additionally, as the videos should be transcoded in real-time, the content of the video streams should be analyzed on a frame-by-frame basis. Thus, analyzing many future frames or even the whole stream before deciding about the current frame is not worth further considerations.

For a fast content analysis on a frame-by-frame basis, we defined different measures and basic tools which solely use the encoded DCT values as well as motion vector information. In section 4.3.1 and 4.3.2, these measures are presented in detail. To show how the defined measures could be used for video content analysis, we developed a fast approach to detect different kinds of scene changes and special movements within MPEG-4 videos in the compressed domain. All details of this approach are presented in section 4.3.3 followed by a short discussion.

4.3.1 Macro Block Analysis

As already described in section 2.1, each MPEG-compressed video frame is divided into 8×8 pixels blocks. Each four neighboring blocks build a macro block (MB) which holds the motion information in the form of one or four motion vectors (MV). In the compressed domain each block contains 8×8 DCT values, i.e., one DC value and 63 AC values. Depending on the frame type and the used motion information, three different macro block types exist:

i) intra-coded macro blocks, which contain only DCT values without any motion information,

ii) inter-coded macro blocks, which contain a residual error, computed by the use of motion vectors pointing into one or two reference frames, and

iii) not coded macro blocks, which do not contain any information.

I-frames do not contain any motion information and therefore, only consist of intra-coded macro blocks. P- and B-frames, in contrast, usually consist of inter-coded macro blocks and may also contain intra-coded macro blocks. Since neither the initial settings nor the performance of the encoder which was used to encode a video stream are known when processing a compressed video stream, one cannot conclude a typical underlying content or specific scene change based on the coding type of the macro blocks only. However, typical encoders prioritize size as a major factor when encoding a video into MPEG-4 video. During this process motion compensation supports the idea of referring to the same content in the vicinity of a macro block in a preceding or succeeding frame. If no macro block with a similar content is found in the surrounding area, the macro block has to be coded as an intra-coded macro block.

For further analysis of the DCT values, we define a complexity measure for the whole frame which is based on the number of non-zero DCT values $n_{\neg 0}$ of all macro blocks:

$$c = \frac{n_{\neg 0}}{64 \cdot n_B} \tag{4.1}$$

with 64 being the number of DCT values in each 8×8 pixels block and n_B being the number of blocks within the frame. The complexity c of a frame can therefore range between 0 and 1 and the lower c the less complex the frame is.

In the case of inter-coded frames, i.e., P- and B-frames, macro blocks may be inter- or intra-coded depending on the decision at encoding time. The ratio of intra- and inter-coded macro blocks of inter-coded frames is of interest, as one can use the information that a block was initially intra-coded as a hint that motion estimation was unsuccessful. Thus, we define a second measure for each frame, based on the macro block types within the frame, which we call the intra-ratio:

$$r_{INTRA} = \frac{n_{MB,INTRA}}{n_{MB}} \tag{4.2}$$

with $n_{MB,INTRA}$ being the number of intra-coded macro blocks in the frame and n_{MB} being the total number of macro blocks in the frame. Based on this hint about unsuccessful motion estimation, the intra-ratio is very handy for detecting scene cuts, which will be seen later on in this section.

4.3.2 Motion Vector Analysis

Motion in videos shall be interpreted as the change or variation of a reference image over time. In this instance, time is split into discrete time codes assigned to individual video frames. By working with a set of full frames, motion can be tracked as the difference between succeeding images. MPEG video makes use of those differences in the encoding process and can track motion by identifying similar content in the vicinity of the previous frame for each macro block. This in return allows for more detailed analysis of the frame. During this search two major cases can be differentiated:

1. The tracking of the same content in a reference frame was *successful* and the motion can be described using a motion vector. This can be the result of two cases:

   - The content looked up is in fact the same as the content from the reference frame.
   - The content matches an area with similar content in the reference frame but from a different scene.

2. The tracking was *unsuccessful* within the analyzed area, which can mainly have two causes:

- The content is not available because the scene has changed or the content has changed too much.

- The content is out of range, meaning it moved too far from its origin position.

Motion Vector Ratio

As we have seen before, not all macro blocks contain motion information in the form of motion vectors. Intra-coded macro blocks do not contain any motion information, and inter-coded macro blocks may contain 1 or 4 motion vectors. MPEG-4 defines 1 or 4 motion vectors per inter-coded macro block. Thus, we can define a third measure for each frame, the motion vector ratio (MV-ratio):

$$r_{mv} = \frac{n_{MV}}{n_{max,MV}}, \qquad with \quad n_{max,MV} = 4\,n_{MB} \tag{4.3}$$

with n_{MV} being the number of non-zero motion vectors in the frame, and $n_{max,MV}$ being the maximum possible number of motion vectors in the frame, calculated by 4 times the number of coded macro blocks (n_{MB}). The motion vector ratio provides information about how many of the possible motion vectors are actually used to describe movements between the previous and the current frame, and it is therefore also a measure for the amount of motion in the frame.

Motion Vector Classification

In order to quickly analyze motion vectors, we define two classification schemes of the non-zero motion vectors within a frame:

- The Cartesian classification scheme maps each motion vector to one rectangular sector which corresponds to its length and direction.

- The polar coordinate classification scheme maps each motion vector to one polar sector which corresponds solely to its direction.

Figure 4.30 illustrates both, the Cartesian classification approach as well as the polar coordinate classification approach. Both approaches have 16 different classes to which all motion vectors are matched, indicated by the numbers in the figures. Each motion vector is mapped to exactly one of these classes, according to its values. The vector indicated by an arrow, for instance, belongs to class 5 in the Cartesian classification and to class number 1 in the polar coordinate scheme. The granularity of both approaches may be extended by introducing more detailed scanning directions and multiple motion vector length classes. However, for our approach, we observed that 16 different vector classes are sufficient to get reasonable results.

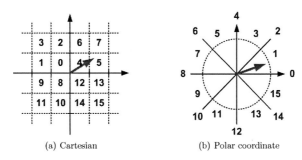

(a) Cartesian   (b) Polar coordinate

Figure 4.30: Motion vector classification schemes

Based on these classification schemes, we can count the number of motion vectors in each class and build a histogram for each scheme of all motion vectors of a frame. However, for detecting special movements in the frames, we should also take into account the origin of each motion vector, since such movements contain motion vectors pointing in opposite directions when observing from the center of the frame. Therefore, we split up the frame into four quadrants resulting in one histogram per quadrant of the frame as shown in figure 4.31(a). The motion vectors of all macro blocks located in one of the four quadrants of the frame are counted in the corresponding histogram. Thus, there are four histograms computed per frame, as indicated in figure 4.31(a). A resulting histogram of a full frame for a potential zoom movement is shown in figure 4.31(b), where the height of each bar illustrates the number of motion vectors in the corresponding class. One can see how most of the motion vectors are orientated in a way, so one would suggest that this frame is part of a zoom movement, since nearly all motion vectors are pointing outwards.

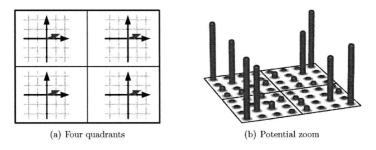

(a) Four quadrants   (b) Potential zoom

Figure 4.31: Frame histogram of a full frame

4.3.3 Scene Change Detection

Scene change detection is an important mechanism for automatic video indexing and segmentation. For video adaptation, the information about scene changes can be used to determine suitable adaptation parameters. When working in the decompressed domain, i.e., the pixel domain, scene changes can be detected by inspecting the pixel values of the video frames as well as the changes between successive frames. However, scene change detection in the decompressed domain is computationally expensive as most video streams are stored in a compressed format. This makes video analysis in the compressed domain the much more favorable option. In the case of MPEG-compressed video, this can be achieved by analyzing the DCT values and the motion information of each frame, which are directly accessible in the compressed domain. Typically, scene changes can be detected by inspecting the differences of successive frames. Due to the nature of MPEG compression, the encoded DCT values and motion vectors of a frame already contain information about these differences. Thus, when working in the compressed domain, we can reuse this available information to decide about the existence of a scene change on a frame-by-frame basis. When analyzing the DCT values as well as the motion information, we can also detect special movements like rotations or zooms within the video stream. For the adaptation of compressed video, the detection of scene changes or special movements can provide helpful information to determine suitable adaptation parameters as well as to decide whether a certain frame should be skipped.

In this section we describe a fast frame-based scene change detection algorithm for MPEG-4 video which is working in the compressed domain and uses the aforementioned measures. For scene change detection we concentrate on P-frames within the video streams. All video sequences which we either used to develop or to evaluate our algorithm were encoded by using only one key frame (i.e., an I-frame) at the beginning and solely P-frames for the rest of the stream. Because I-frames do not contain any motion information, our algorithm cannot definitely decide whether such a frame belongs to a scene change or not. However, most encoders already use basic scene change detection mechanisms and for those video streams which are encoded with a minimum number of I-frames it is very likely that an I-frame is a cut between two scenes. For the case that the video stream also contains B-frames, our algorithm can be easily extended by some modifications of its parameters. For such bidirectionally predicted frames the thresholds that we identified for the proposed measures in case of P-frames need to be adjusted for B-frames. Additionally, as B-frames may contain both forward and backward motion vectors, the motion vector histograms need to be computed for both directions.

There are a couple of basic scene changes and special movements that can be observed in many videos. Figure 4.32 illustrates some of them. These basic scene changes and movements are not always present as stand-alone movements but rather as a combination of multiple changes.

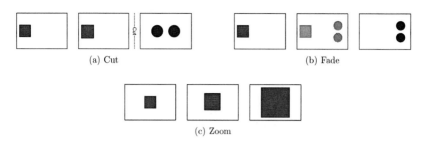

Figure 4.32: Different scene changes and special movements

The basic changes and movements considered in this section are:

a) Scene *cuts*, which result in different content compared to the previous frame.

b) Scene *fades*, which are frames providing a transition between two reference frames A and B. Each of the fade frames is a frame $C = x_a \cdot A + x_b \cdot B$ with x_a, x_b being an intensity measure to describe the portion being added from each of the reference frames. $0 \leq x_a, x_b \leq 1$ with $x_a + x_b = 1$.

c) Movements in the form of a *zoom*, which means that a portion of a frame is magnified or demagnified.

We developed our scene change detection algorithm by inspecting the previously defined measures and histograms for several video sequences from a variety of different genres and with different content. We used ten different video sequences, which are freely available on the Internet, ranging from movie trailers to merchandise videos with different characteristics. For each test video, we firstly analyzed the position of scene changes and special movements in the sequence by visual inspection. Afterwards, we computed the values of the complexity, the intra-ratio, and the motion vector ratio of each frame. By analyzing these values in combination with the position of the scene changes, we got different thresholds for existing scene changes and special movements. By this comprehensive analysis, we found, for instance, a threshold for the motion vector ratio, that can be used to decide whether or not a given frame belongs to any scene change. Our test showed that if the motion vector ratio of a frame is below 0.3, it does not belong to any of the considered scene changes or movements. In the following sections we describe the other thresholds, which we got from our analysis, as well as our scene change detection algorithm for the aforementioned scene changes and movements.

Existing Approaches

As described by Boreczky et al. [100] there has been a lot of research work on video segmentation and scene change detection. Several approaches are working in the uncompressed domain such as those described in [101, 102, 103, 104, 105]. It is important to mention that some of these approaches use very specific and situation-related knowledge about the video content, such as for detecting scene changes in video coverage of sporting events by Han et al. [105]. Some papers can be found which are decoding only a low resolution version of each frame [106, 107, 108, 109] and therefore avoid the complexity of a complete decoding. Another set of papers deals with analyzing stored video sequences in the compressed domain by inspecting the differences of successive frames [110, 111] and by using several statistical tests [112, 113] for scene change detection.

Pei et al. proposed an algorithm which uses the macro block type for detection of wipe effects in the compressed domain [114]. Wipe effects are gradual transitions from one scene to another, which are widely used in video editing. However, due to the highly artificial nature of wipe effects, this approach cannot be used for general scene change detection. Analyzing information from the motion vectors in the compressed domain has been done for several versions of MPEG video [115, 116]. The idea of using a combination of multiple cues, which are based on motion vectors and macro block information, was presented by Troller et al. in [117]. However, the computations needed to derive these cues still use information from the decompressed domain. Our approach incorporates this idea of combining motion vector and DCT value analysis, but it completely avoids the use of decoded information and therefore saves the processing time needed for video decoding.

In a way, our approach is of minimalistic nature so that the video in question does not need to be decoded at all. Furthermore, we use metrics and motion vector histograms that are easy to compute, and therefore our algorithm needs only a minimum of processing time for detecting scene changes and special movements. The primary objective of our algorithm design is speed and minimal workload for analysis and decision making. As our approach does not need to compare consecutive frames or compute statistical tests, it has a much lower complexity than those compressed domain approaches mentioned before. The video format in question shall be MPEG-4, and the following sections will only refer to the macro blocks, the motion vectors, and the AC and DC values from the DCT in their coded form. As quality and accuracy of the scene change detection shall be of interest as well, speed and easy computation of a decision are foremost important because our approach is targeted for solutions that are providing video adaptation for mobile devices with limited resources.

Cut Detection

In the case of scene cuts, the contents of the frames before and after the cut differ completely, which is schematically illustrated in figure 4.32(a). Therefore, a cut within a video is quite easy to detect by inspecting the intra-ratio of a frame as described in equation 4.2. The first frame of the new scene is normally identified by a high ratio of intra-coded macro blocks. Typical numbers are around 0.50 to 0.60, but might range up to 0.99. It is important to mention that it is always above the average intra-ratio of previous frames. Additionally, the complexity c, which was computed by equation 4.1, is also much higher than that of an average frame.

For most inter-coded frames in our test videos, that belong to a cut, the intra-ratio was above 0.5 combined with a complexity higher than 0.04. However, there were also a couple of cut-related frames with a much higher complexity but slightly lower intra-ratio. By inspecting the complexity and intra-ratio of such frames, we got the alternative thresholds of 0.4 for the intra-ratio and 0.08 for the complexity, which can be used to identify the remaining cuts. Therefore, two combinations of thresholds are being proposed, and each frame with parameters above one of these combined thresholds is considered a cut. Additionally, we observed a motion vector ratio higher than 0.95 in almost all frames of scene cuts. Only in a few situations this was not true but we observed that the motion vector ratio was still at least 40 % above the average ratio calculated for the previous five frames. Thus, the detection of scene changes can be summarized as:

$$
\begin{aligned}
isCut = & \Big((c > 0.04 \ \wedge \ r_{INTRA} > 0.5) \quad \vee \quad (c > 0.08 \ \wedge \ r_{INTRA} > 0.4) \Big) \ \bigwedge \\
& (r_{mv} > 0.95 \ \vee \ r_{mv} > 1.4 \, r_{mv,avg})
\end{aligned} \tag{4.4}
$$

with c, r_{INTRA} and r_{mv} as described in section 4.3.1 and the average MV-ratio $r_{mv,avg}$ of the previous five frames. The use of the MV-ratio in this equation indicates that we need to store some information about previous frames for our scene change detection approach. This can be achieved by simply calculating and storing the moving average of the MV-ratio.

Fade Detection

Fades within a video stream are transitions from one scene to the next scene and stretch over a couple of frames. A fade can basically be described as the addition of two images, namely the source and target images, with different factors. While the first image shows 100 % of the source image, following images show a higher and higher percentage of the target image intensity-wise until reaching 100 % of the target image. This case is schematically illustrated in figure 4.32(b). The content of the source and target image, however, might be a moving image itself and lead to an overlay of content-related and fade-related changes. This makes it more complicated to define a fade as such.

Our observations showed that, compared to the average parameters of the whole video, the motion vector ratio is above average values and the complexity is not that high in situations of a fade, if the source and target videos are still images and do not move much themselves. Then the only motion resulting is the transition between the images. Our analysis of the test sequences also showed that a typical pattern can be observed in the described parameters as well as in the motion vector histograms. Nevertheless, due to the nature of natural video this pattern is not continuous over the period of the whole fade. Typical fades last between 10 and 50 frames, and identifying patterns such as a high MV-ratio and medium complexity can only be observed in the majority but not in all of the frames. As the detection should be done on a frame-by-frame basis, fades are therefore quite hard to detect.

For most frames that belong to a fade in our test videos the complexity was around the range of 0.01 to 0.16. This wide range is one of the main reasons which makes it difficult to come to a qualified decision. Naturally, the complexity changes with increased quantizer scale values as well, so the values shown here are only valid for the range of quantizer scale values between 1 and around 5. However, it is possible to reduce the threshold in the same way as for any other complexity measure, which is decreasing with increasing quantizer scale values. Additionally, the MV-ratio as well as the intra-ratio provide some additional hints for fade detection. For our test sequences, the MV-ratio of frames, which belong to a fade, was around 0.9 and not lower than 0.8. The intra-ratio for such frames was between 0.1 and 0.4. For fade detection, we combined the complexity, the intra-ratio, and the MV-ratio, so that nearly all of the frames, which belong to a fade in our test sequences, satisfied the following equation.

$$isFade = (c + r_{INTRA}) > 0.22 \ \wedge \ r_{INTRA} > 0.15 \ \wedge \ r_{mv} > 0.8 \qquad (4.5)$$

with c, r_{INTRA} and r_{mv} as described in section 4.3.1.

Observations in some of our test videos showed that some special movements such as explosions or sparkling bubbles in a water tank are also detected as fades. The reason for this effect is that in both cases we there are similar divergent movements within the video frames as there would be in the case of fading from one scene to another. Therefore, it is quite obvious that our approach cannot differentiate between them.

Zoom Detection

A zoom is a camera operation that either enlarges an area of an image, or in the opposite direction, gets more information about the area surrounding the original image, where the original image is a subset of the zoomed image. Figure 4.32(c), for instance, shows an enlarging zoom. Thus, we can assume that most of the motion vectors of a frame which belongs to a zoom are pointing outwards or inwards. In order to detect such a zoom, we use the motion vector histograms and count the number of motion vectors in classes of outwards or inwards pointing vectors respectively.

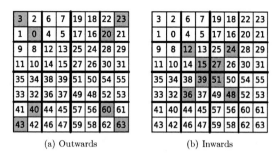

(a) Outwards   (b) Inwards

Figure 4.33: Motion vector classes for zoom detection

Figures 4.33(a) and 4.33(b) each show the 8 zoom indicative classes of outwards and inwards pointing vectors in the Cartesian histogram which we used to detect zooms. For the polar coordinate histogram we have 12 classes for each case. From our test video analysis we know that those frames belonging to a zoom, have a MV-ratio above 0.4. Therefore, we consider those vectors pointing outwards or inwards to be zoom indicative only if the motion vector ratio of the current frame is above 0.4. To decide whether a frame belongs to a zoom or not, some further inspection of the zoom indicative motion vectors is needed. For our test videos, the number of zoom indicative vectors of most frames which were part of a zoom were more than 30 % higher than the expected value for both the Cartesian and the polar coordinate histogram. For the rest of zoom frames, the number of zoom indicative vectors were 100 % higher than the expected value either for the Cartesian or for the polar coordinate histogram. The expected value is hereby calculated as $\frac{n_z}{64} n_{mv}$ with n_z being the number of zoom indicative classes, 64 being the number of all classes, and n_{mv} being the number of non zero motion vectors. For the Cartesian histogram, n_z has the value of 8 (see figure 4.33), and for the polar coordinate histogram the values is 12. With these values we can summarize the detection of a zoom as follows.

$$isZoom = r_{mv} > 0.4 \bigwedge \Big(\ (n_{z,C} > 1.3 \, \tfrac{1}{8} \, n_{mv} \quad \wedge \quad n_{z,P} > 1.3 \, \tfrac{3}{16} \, n_{mv}) \ \bigvee$$
$$(n_{z,C} > \tfrac{1}{4} \, n_{mv} \quad \vee \quad n_{z,P} > \tfrac{3}{8} \, n_{mv}) \qquad \Big) \qquad (4.6)$$

with r_{mv} as described in section 4.3.1, as well as $n_{z,C}$ and $n_{z,P}$ as the number of zoom indicative motion vectors for the Cartesian and polar coordinate histogram, respectively.

Detection of other movements

Similarly to the detection of zooms, the motion vector histograms may also be used to detect further movements within video streams, such as translations or rotations. A translation is a unidirectional movement in either x- or y-direction, like a camera turn left or right. A rotation is a movement that is predominantly directed clock-wise or anti-clockwise, and may result from rotating the camera or from a rotating object. For both movements, we observed an increased motion vector ratio for those frames of our test videos, which show such a movement. For a translation, we observed a very high ratio at about 0.9 and above, and for a rotation we observed a ratio above 0.7. However, for the movements in our test videos that we identified as a translation or rotation by visual inspection, we could not find a clear pattern for the motion vector histograms. The reason for that is, that such movements as described above are idealized and simplified. In existing video sequences, there are often combinations of such movements or they cannot be clearly identified by the viewer. In contrast to zoom movements, translations and rotations are not always aligned to the center of the frame, which makes the definition of a clear motion vector pattern very hard. Therefore, we limited our scene change detection approach to cut, fade, and zoom detection.

Evaluation

The scene change detection algorithm was implemented based on the processing architecture which was presented in section 4.2.3. We implemented our presented methods as one transcoding module of the multidimensional transcoder. This module analyzes each frame by building the presented motion vector histograms and computing the aforementioned measures. Based on this information, it decides for each frame whether it belongs to a scene change or to a special movement in the video stream.

For the evaluation of our scene detection algorithm, we selected video sequences which differ from those we used for the development of this algorithm. The selected sequences differ in spatial resolution as well as in the amount and type of motion within the sequences. We used two movie trailers with a high number of cuts and fades, one sequence from TV news with a low number of cuts, fades and zooms, and one sequence from a soccer game with only a few cuts and fades but a higher number of zooms. The spatial resolution of these sequences ranges from 320×240 pixels to 1280×720 pixels and the duration of each sequence was 90 seconds. All evaluation sequences were encoded by using a slightly modified version of the MPEG-4 codec included in FFmpeg. This modification was necessary, as FFmpeg already has a rudimentary build-in scene change detection algorithm, which inserts an I-frame whenever a scene change is detected. For the evaluation of our scene change detection algorithm, we simply disabled this insertion of extra I-frames. With this modified version of FFmpeg, we got video streams which only consist of one single I-frame as the first frame, followed solely by P-frames.

Table 4.9 shows the results of our evaluation. For each of the test videos the number of existing, detected and falsely detected scene changes and movements are shown. The news sequence, for instance, contained 14 scene cuts, from which 13 were detected by our algorithm, and in two cases our algorithm detected a cut although no scene change was present. All existing fades and zooms in the test sequences were detected correctly and there were a few single frames which were falsely detected as such movements. However, we can assume that fades and zooms last for at least two or three frames. Therefore, the detection of single frames as belonging to a fade or zoom can be easily eliminated and therefore is not shown in the table.

Video	Cut	Fade	Zoom
	existing/detected/false positives		
news	14/13/2	1/1/2	2/2/0
soccer	4/4/1	5/5/3	9/7/0
movie-1	51/48/1	8/7/4	3/3/0
movie-2	49/38/11	14/13/2	7/7/0

Table 4.9: Evaluation results

Although there are some false positive detections for cuts and fades, the results are very promising. Moreover, most of the falsely detected frames can be explained quite easily because they either belong to one of the two other types of scene cuts and movements, or they belong to another special movement not covered by our algorithm. For instance, 9 out of 11 falsely detected scene cuts of the movie-2 sequence actually belong to a fast fade and in 2 frames the colour of the background changes from one frame to another which could also be interpreted as a cut. On the other hand, 8 of the undetected scene cuts in movie-2 were detected as a fade and only 3 frames were not detected as any type of scene change. Another example are the 3 falsely detected fades in the soccer sequence. They result from a high amount of movement of the background whereas the moving person in the foreground remains in the focus of the camera and therefore relatively stable in the middle of the frame.

At the bottom line, it can be stated that the presented algorithm detects the existence of a scene change or special movement quite reliably although the type of movement involved cannot always be identified correctly. The average processing time per frame of our proposed scene change detection algorithm ranges from 0.6 to 6.5 ms for the test videos which is about 18 % to 33 % of the processing time needed for parsing the video bit stream. Related to the duration of the video streams, the analysis consumed between 2 % of the processing time for the streams with the lowest spatial resolution (320×240 pixels) and 19 % for the stream with the highest spatial resolution (1280×720 pixels).

4.3.4 Discussion

In this section we have presented different measures that can be used for compressed domain content analysis for digital video streams. The usability of these measures was shown by the presentation of a fast frame-based algorithm for compressed domain scene change detection in MPEG-4 video streams. This algorithm analyzes the DCT values and motion vectors of each frame in order to decide whether this frame belongs to a scene change or special movement. As a basis for this decision, we defined three different measures as well as two different motion vector classification schemes which are used by our algorithm. The fast and easy computation of the used metrics and histograms makes the whole scene change detection algorithm very fast which is an important aspect for real time video processing.

The highly statistical nature of the scene change detection results in a statement that by design cannot be absolutely correct. Therefore, the scene change detection can only be a tool to indicate a stronger or weaker correlation towards one or the other scene movement. However, the evaluation results show that the algorithm detects a high number of scene changes and movements.

In the context of multidimensional compressed domain video transcoding the presented scene change detection algorithm could be used to dynamically control the transcoding parameters. For the frame skipping transcoder, for instance, the algorithm could be used to decide whether a certain frame should be skipped or not. Skipping the first frame after a scene cut, for instance, would result in a high transcoding error that could be avoided by skipping any of the following frames instead. Also in situations with fast and high amounts of motion, such as in the case of a zoom or a fast fading scene, the transcoder may benefit from the information that is generated by using the scene change detection algorithm.

4.4 Summary

In this chapter we presented our research on multidimensional video transcoding as a new approach for video adaptation for mobile devices. Based on our analysis of the impact of different video characteristics such as spatial or temporal resolution, on the resource requirements that a receiving device has to comply with, we identified three adaptation dimensions that are essential to support a great heterogeneity of mobile devices. These dimensions are: the spatial, the temporal, and the detail resolution. In the literature these dimensions are typically treated separately as we have shown in chapter 2. Therefore, we analyzed how an adaptation of these dimensions affects the produced quality in terms of PSNR values as well as by using a subjective quality assessment for temporal adaptation.

This analysis clearly showed that any kind of combined adaptation should start with tailoring the spatial resolution of a video stream to the display resolution of the requesting device. If further bit rate reduction is needed, the frame rate should be reduced by a factor of two. Finally, the detail resolution could be reduced by using a higher quantizer scale value to further reduce the bit rate.

In order to achieve this kind of multidimensional adaptation, we presented a novel multidimensional transcoding approach that smartly combines existing one-dimensional compressed domain transcoders into a transcoder chain. Therefore, we decomposed a frame-skipping, a downscaling, and a requantization transcoder into several transcoder modules. Additionally, we developed a processing architecture that allows a new composition of these decomposed transcoder modules. Afterwards, we presented our prototype implementation of a three-dimensional transcoder for MPEG-4 video streams. For each dimension we implemented and evaluated several different refinement methods. The evaluation of our MPEG-4 transcoder with respect to the produced quality proved the usability of the presented multidimensional transcoding approach. The transcoded video streams showed comparable or even better results than the recoded streams.

In the analysis of different adaptation dimensions we identified that some adaptation parameters may depend on the actual content of the processed video stream. Therefore, we developed different measures that allow a content analysis of video streams in the compressed domain. By using these measures for a fast frame-based scene change detection algorithm, we proved the relevance of these measures for video content analysis. Additionally, the compressed domain scene change detection algorithm can be used during the transcoding process, for instance, to decide whether a frame should be skipped or not.

Chapter 5

Conclusion and Outlook

The rapid development in the area of mobile devices in combination with an increasing network bandwidth for Internet access in the last years makes multimedia services available to a great range of different devices in a variety of situations. Especially the developments in the areas of wireless network connectivity enable the users of mobile devices to access a huge number of multimedia streams available on the Internet.

However, there are still essential hardware or software related issues of mobile devices as well as problems related to the transmission of multimedia streams over a wireless network connection. Some of these issues were discussed in this thesis. Mobile devices, for instance, typically have only limited resources available and are therefore not always capable of processing and displaying all those different video streams. Even if the receiving device has enough resources it may still lack support of the video format. The wireless connection may additionally limit the experience of video streaming compared to a wired connection. If several devices share the same medium on a wireless link, the throughput will be lower for each single device, and interferences on the wireless link may result in packet loss which again reduces the visual quality of the stream.

Content providers typically aim at serving all these different requirements that result from the network connectivity and the device capabilities. Therefore, they may need to provide different versions of each video stream. As this solution produces additional storage costs for the provider, it is favorable to provide only one high quality version of each video stream and then individually adapt these streams as needed for each requesting client.

However, an adaptation of video data on the mobile devices themselves is unsuitable due to their limited resources as well as the typically limited network capacity on the wireless link. Instead such an adaptation needs to be located on an involved network node, for instance, either at an intermediate gateway or directly at the media server. The gateway-based solution is the most flexible one as it makes the adaptation service usable for all accessible video streams on all reachable media servers. The heterogeneity of mobile devices and the complexity of digital video streams make individual video adaptation a challenging task as several different parameters and adaptation dimensions need to be considered to achieve a reasonable quality.

5.1 Contributions

The central idea of our work on multidimensional transcoding arises from the observation that the characteristics as well as the visual quality of digital video streams result from a variety of different aspects and parameters. The bit rate of a video stream, for instance, does not solely result from the spatial resolution of the video frames, but also from other parameters like the frame rate, the detail resolution, the encoding format and the amount of motion in the stream. Thus, an adaptation of a video stream can be achieved in different dimensions by tailoring some or all of these parameters. Our contributions towards adaptive multimedia streaming can be summarized as:

- the identification of the spatial, the temporal and the detail dimension as the essential characteristics of digital video streams as well as the analysis of the impact of their adaptation on the visual quality of video streams;

- the recommendation of an approach for multidimensional video adaptation that includes adaptation of the spatial, the temporal as well as the detail resolution of video streams;

- the presentation of a smart combination of different compressed domain transcoding techniques in order to support a great heterogeneity of different devices;

- the design and implementation of an integrated and flexible processing architecture for multidimensional compressed domain video transcoding;

- the development and implementation of a three-dimensional MPEG-4 video transcoder which is able to adapt digital video streams for mobile devices within the spatial, the temporal and the detail dimension;

- the development of different measures for content analysis of video streams in the compressed domain;

- the development of a fast frame-based algorithm for compressed domain scene change detection in MPEG-4 video streams;

- the design and implementation of a comprehensive architecture of a multimedia gateway system that can load different adaptation libraries at runtime and thereby provide multimedia adaptation services to requesting clients;

- the integration of further features into the developed multimedia gateway that enhance the functionality and usability of the proposed gateway system: flexible stream reflection, automatic gateway discovery, integrated capability exchange, session transfer as well as cooperative caching.

In this work we analyzed the impact of different video adaptation dimensions on the resource requirements at the receiving device. We identified three main dimensions that a video adaptation service for mobile devices should support. These are the temporal resolution, the spatial resolution as well as the detail resolution of a video stream. We presented an analysis of the visual quality that can be achieved by tailoring video streams in these three dimensions. Based on this analysis, we further proposed a clear recommendation for a multidimensional approach to the adaptation of digital video streams for mobile devices: Primarily, the spatial resolution of a stream should be tailored to the display resolution of the client. If further reduction of the bit rate is needed, the frame rate of the stream should be reduced, for instance, to the half of the original rate. Finally, the detail resolution should be used to fine tune the bit rate of the stream to the available bandwidth of the network connection.

For the adaptation process itself, we concentrated on compressed domain video transcoding techniques as key technologies for video adaptation. Compared to pixel domain transcoding, compressed domain video transcoding can significantly reduce the processing power needed for video adaptation by avoiding a complete decoding and encoding of the video stream. Existing transcoding approaches as proposed in the literature, however, concentrate on adaptation of video streams solely in one single dimension or tailor the streams only for some limited scenarios. Therefore, in this thesis we analyzed how existing transcoding mechanisms could be combined to build a multidimensional transcoder that supports individual fine-grained video adaptation for mobile devices. Based on this analysis, we presented a novel approach that smartly combines different existing one-dimensional compressed domain transcoding techniques and builds a transcoder chain that provides multidimensional video transcoding. By the use of this approach, we implemented a multidimensional MPEG-4 transcoder that is working completely in the compressed domain to demonstrate the usability of our approach. The evaluation of this prototype implementation shows that the produced quality is comparable to the quality produced by a cascaded decoder and encoder working in the pixel domain or even better in some cases. This also proves the functionality of the proposed multidimensional transcoder architecture. To the best of our knowledge, this thesis is the first work that proposes such a flexible video transcoding architecture for multidimensional video adaptation.

The bit rate of a video stream at a certain quality level is mainly controlled by the amount of motion and details contained in the particular stream. The amount of motion and details, however, typically is not constant during a video sequence with a duration of more than a few seconds but varies over time and depends on the content of the video stream. Our analysis of the impact of the temporal resolution on the visual quality of the stream showed that the content of a video stream also has an impact on the frame rate that is preferred by the user. Therefore, we proposed different measures that allow for a fast and frame-based content analysis directly in the compressed domain. Since these measures can be computed very fast, they are well suited to be used in a compressed domain transcoder to get some additional information about the content of the current video stream without any further decoding overhead. The usability of these measures was shown in a novel scene change detection algorithm that is working completely in the compressed domain.

In order to make the proposed multidimensional video transcoding available to mobile devices, we proposed a comprehensive multimedia gateway architecture. This architecture supports to dynamically load different adaptation libraries at runtime and therefore, provides an individual video adaptation service to mobile clients. Further features of our gateway system include: stream reflection, gateway discovery, capability exchange, session transfer and cooperative caching. The flexible stream reflection feature of the gateway can be used for application layer multicast or collaborative streaming scenarios where all connected clients should receive their individually tailored stream. Furthermore, before a client can use any gateway, the proposed gateway discovery mechanism can be used to let the client discover or request for an appropriate gateway. The described capability exchange mechanism that is embedded in the RTSP communication can be used to send information about the client capabilities to the gateway that can load the appropriate adaptation library to adapt the requested stream. The caching ability of our gateway architecture helps to reduce the startup delay at the client for cached streams and additionally reduces the network load between the gateways in the access network and the media server on the Internet. By the use of all these features, our gateway architecture is able to provide video adaptation services to its clients that can be used very easily and without additional user interaction as all additional communication is done automatically. To the best of our knowledge, no comparable multimedia gateway system could be found in the literature that combines all these features in one comprehensive system.

5.2 Open Issues and Future Work

By the use of the processing architecture presented in this work, powerful multidimensional transcoders can be build. These transcoders can be used on multimedia gateways such as the one proposed in this thesis. By the combination of both, i.e., a multimedia gateway system that provides a multidimensional video transcoding service to mobile clients, a significant service enhancement for users with mobile devices can be achieved. Nevertheless, there is still room for improvements and further research. In the following sections, we provide some ideas for further research directions.

5.2.1 Combining Transcoding and Scalable Video Coding

The concept of scalable or layered video coding is an approach to digital video coding that provides video scalability in different dimensions. The adaptation of scalable video streams is quite simple as single layers can be discarded without influencing the decoding process of the remaining lower layers. As discussed in section 2.3.2, scalable video streams are still hardly used in Internet based video streaming and scalable video coding also has some drawbacks that make single layer video adaptation still necessary. Moreover, both technologies, scalable video coding as well as video transcoding, meet different needs for different application scenarios, and therefore likely will coexist in the near future as presented by Vetro in [118]. Besides this coexistence, it may be worthwhile to combine both technologies to provide individual video streaming to mobile devices. Park et al., for instance, proposed to use transcoding mechanisms to enable random access for scalable encoded video streams in [119]. Another example is an approach, proposed by De Cock et al. in [120] to transcode single layer MPEG-4 AVC video streams to SVC streams. Both examples show that using video transcoding techniques to create or to enhance a scalable video stream is possible and can be beneficial.

Based on these examples of a simple combination of transcoding mechanisms and scalable video coding, a further research direction would be to investigate how to combine both approaches efficiently. Research could investigate how to minimize the overhead introduced by scalable video coding on the one hand while at the same time aiming at the minimization of the processing time needed for transcoding on the other hand, and additionally, still remain a good perceived visual quality for the user of the receiving device.

5.2.2 Transcoding and Digital Rights Management

In the context of multimedia streaming, content providers need to respect the copyright of the provided video streams. In case that the receiver pays for receiving the content, the provider typically needs to limit the usage of the video sequence to the receiver only. For this purpose, several different methods exist which prevent the usage of digital video streams for any other purpose that the streams are not intended for by the provider. A common term for these methods is the digital rights management (DRM).

In the context of video adaptation, any instance that may adapt the video stream to the requirements of the client needs to access the content of the video stream. In the case that the video stream is protected by some DRM methods, this access to the content is typically only possible for the receiving client and not for any other or intermediate system. The proposed transcoder as well as all other transcoding architectures currently are not able to adapt such protected video streams. Thus, another research direction may be to investigate the possibilities to enable video adaptation for DRM protected video streams.

5.2.3 Audio Adaptation

In the introduction to this thesis we stated that our focus is on adaptive video streaming whereas the adaptation of audio streams is out of scope of this work. The audio information, however, is typically more important to the user than the video stream. Thus, for adaptation of multimedia content, the audio streams may need to be adapted to the requirements of the client as well. As audio streams are less complex than video streams and typically consume only a fraction of the bandwidth compared to the video streams, an adaptation could be achieved by combining a cascaded decoder and encoder. The more important and demanding aspect in the context of audio adaptation may therefore be the question, which kind of adaptation produces the best quality of experience for the user. Additionally, it may be interesting to analyze the results of a combined audio and video adaptation.

5.2.4 Optimization

A more practical open issue is the optimization of the current transcoder implementation. Since the transcoder implementation presented in this thesis was developed from scratch, there is some room for optimization in terms of processing time needed for video adaptation. This can be achieved by optimizing the existing code as well as by implementing more advanced transcoding techniques. One example of the latter kind of optimization would be the replacement of the implemented straight forward inverse motion compensation by one of those approaches mentioned in the discussion of our transcoder implementation.

Appendix A

Implementation Details

A.1 CC/PP Schema for Client Profiles

In this section we provide a CC/PP schema that defines a profile containing device capabilities as well as user preferences, which can be used to select an appropriate adaptation method at a multimedia gateway. A profile contains up to four different components that are called *Hardware, Software, User* and *Priority*. This schema was developed based on an example schema given in the User Agent Profiling Specification [121].

```
<?xml version="1.0" encoding="utf-8"?>

<rdf:RDF xmlns:rdf="http://www.w3.org/1999/02/22-rdf-syntax-ns#"
         xmlns:rdfs="http://www.w3.org/2000/01/rdf-schema#">

  <rdf:Description rdf:ID="Component">
    <rdf:type rdf:resource="http://www.w3.org/2000/01/rdf-schema#Class"/>
    <rdfs:subClassOf rdf:resource="http://www.w3.org/2000/01/rdf-schema#Resource"/>
    <rdfs:label>Component</rdfs:label>
    <rdfs:comment>
      A Component within the CC/PP schema is a class of related properties that
      describes the capabilities and preferences.
    </rdfs:comment>
  </rdf:Description>

  <!-- ***** Properties shared among the components ***** -->
  <rdf:Description rdf:ID="component">
    <rdf:type rdf:resource="http://www.w3.org/1999/02/22-rdf-syntax-ns#Property"/>
    <rdfs:label>component</rdfs:label>
    <rdfs:comment>
      The component attribute links the various components to the root node (profile).
    </rdfs:comment>
  </rdf:Description>

  <!-- ***** Component Definitions ***** -->
  <rdf:Description rdf:ID="Hardware">
    <rdf:type rdf:resource="http://www.w3.org/2000/01/rdf-schema#Class"/>
    <rdfs:subClassOf rdf:resource="#Component"/>
    <rdfs:label>Component: Hardware</rdfs:label>
    <rdfs:comment>
      The Hardware component contains properties of the device's
      Hardware, such as display size, color depth, etc.
    </rdfs:comment>
  </rdf:Description>
```

```
<rdf:Description rdf:ID="Software">
  <rdf:type rdf:resource="http://www.w3.org/2000/01/rdf-schema#Class"/>
  <rdfs:subClassOf rdf:resource="#Component"/>
  <rdfs:label>Component: Software</rdfs:label>
  <rdfs:comment>
    The Software component contains properties of the device's
    application environment, operating system, and installed software.
    This may also include the information about usable Codecs.
  </rdfs:comment>
</rdf:Description>


<rdf:Description rdf:ID="User">
  <rdf:type rdf:resource="http://www.w3.org/2000/01/rdf-schema#Class"/>
  <rdfs:subClassOf rdf:resource="#Component"/>
  <rdfs:label>Component: User</rdfs:label>
  <rdfs:comment>
    The User component contains user's constraints and wishes,
    which allow a specialized adaption of the media.
  </rdfs:comment>
</rdf:Description>


<rdf:Description rdf:ID="Priority">
  <rdf:type rdf:resource="http://www.w3.org/2000/01/rdf-schema#Class"/>
  <rdfs:subClassOf rdf:resource="#Component"/>
  <rdfs:label>Component: Priority</rdfs:label>
  <rdfs:comment>
    The Priority component caontains user's constraints regarding the
    importance of the attributs given in the other components.
    Values can be ranged from (not important) 0..100 (very important).
  </rdfs:comment>
</rdf:Description>


<!-- **
    ** In the following property definitions, the defined types
    ** are as follows:
    **    Number:     A positive integer     [0-9]+
    **    Boolean:    A yes or no value       Yes|No
    **    Literal:    An alphanumeric string  [A-Za-z0-9/.\-_]+
  -->


<!-- ***** Component: Hardware ***** -->
<rdf:Description rdf:ID="CPU">
  <rdf:type rdf:resource="http://www.w3.org/1999/02/22-rdf-syntax-ns#Property"/>
  <rdfs:domain rdf:resource="#Hardware"/>
  <rdfs:comment>
    Description:  Name and model number of the device CPU.
    Type:         Literal
    Examples:     "Pentium III", "PowerPC 750"
  </rdfs:comment>
</rdf:Description>


<rdf:Description rdf:ID="CPUFrequency">
  <rdf:type rdf:resource="http://www.w3.org/1999/02/22-rdf-syntax-ns#Property"/>
  <rdfs:domain rdf:resource="#Hardware"/>
  <rdfs:comment>
    Description:  Frequency of the device CPU in MHz.
    Type:         Number
    Examples:     "166", 300"
  </rdfs:comment>
</rdf:Description>
```

```
<rdf:Description rdf:ID="Memory">
  <rdf:type rdf:resource="http://www.w3.org/1999/02/22-rdf-syntax-ns#Property"/>
  <rdfs:domain rdf:resource="#Hardware"/>
  <rdfs:comment>
    Description:  The size of the device's memory in MB.
    Type:         Number
    Examples:     "8", "64"
  </rdfs:comment>
</rdf:Description>

<rdf:Description rdf:ID="Model">
  <rdf:type rdf:resource="http://www.w3.org/1999/02/22-rdf-syntax-ns#Property"/>
  <rdfs:domain rdf:resource="#Hardware"/>
  <rdfs:comment>
    Description:  Model number assigned to the terminal device by the vendor.
    Type:         Literal
    Examples:     "N70", "MT50"
  </rdfs:comment>
</rdf:Description>

<rdf:Description rdf:ID="DisplayHeight">
  <rdf:type rdf:resource="http://www.w3.org/1999/02/22-rdf-syntax-ns#Property"/>
  <rdfs:domain rdf:resource="#Hardware"/>
  <rdfs:comment>
    Description:  The height of the device's screen in units of pixels.
    Type:         Number
    Examples:     "160", "640"
  </rdfs:comment>
</rdf:Description>

<rdf:Description rdf:ID="DisplayWidth">
  <rdf:type rdf:resource="http://www.w3.org/1999/02/22-rdf-syntax-ns#Property"/>
  <rdfs:domain rdf:resource="#Hardware"/>
  <rdfs:comment>
    Description:  The width of the device's screen in units of pixels.
    Type:         Number
    Examples:     "160", "480"
  </rdfs:comment>
</rdf:Description>

<rdf:Description rdf:ID="Vendor">
  <rdf:type rdf:resource="http://www.w3.org/1999/02/22-rdf-syntax-ns#Property"/>
  <rdfs:domain rdf:resource="#Hardware"/>
  <rdfs:comment>
    Description:  Name of the vendor manufacturing the terminal device.
    Type:         Literal
    Examples:     "Nokia", "Siemens"
  </rdfs:comment>
</rdf:Description>

<rdf:Description rdf:ID="MaxFrames">
  <rdf:type rdf:resource="http://www.w3.org/1999/02/22-rdf-syntax-ns#Property"/>
  <rdfs:domain rdf:resource="#Hardware"/>
  <rdfs:comment>
    Description:  Specifies the maximum frame rate possible for the device.
                  Values are given in frames per second.
    Type:         Number
    Examples:     "25", "30"
  </rdfs:comment>
</rdf:Description>
```

```
<rdf:Description rdf:ID="Colors">
  <rdf:type rdf:resource="http://www.w3.org/1999/02/22-rdf-syntax-ns#Property"/>
  <rdfs:domain rdf:resource="#Hardware"/>
  <rdfs:comment>
    Description:  Specifies the number of possible colors for the display.
    Type:        Number
    Examples:    "256", "65535"
  </rdfs:comment>
</rdf:Description>

<rdf:Description rdf:ID="MaxAudioRate">
  <rdf:type rdf:resource="http://www.w3.org/1999/02/22-rdf-syntax-ns#Property"/>
  <rdfs:domain rdf:resource="#Hardware"/>
  <rdfs:comment>
    Description:  This value represents the maximal audio data rate that can be
                 processed by the device. The value is expressed in kbit/s;
    Type:        Number
    Examples:    "64", "1024"
  </rdfs:comment>
</rdf:Description>

<rdf:Description rdf:ID="MaxVideoRate">
  <rdf:type rdf:resource="http://www.w3.org/1999/02/22-rdf-syntax-ns#Property"/>
  <rdfs:domain rdf:resource="#Hardware"/>
  <rdfs:comment>
    Description:  This value represents the maximal video data rate that can be
                 processed by the device. The value is expressed in kbit/s.
    Type:        Number
    Examples:    "64", "2048"
  </rdfs:comment>
</rdf:Description>

<rdf:Description rdf:ID="MaxDataRate">
  <rdf:type
    rdf:resource="http://www.w3.org/1999/02/22-rdf-syntax-ns#Property"/>
  <rdfs:domain rdf:resource="#Hardware"/>
  <rdfs:comment>
    Description:  This value represents the maximal data rate that can be
                 received by the device. The value is expressed in kbit/s.
    Type:        Number
    Examples:    "64", "2048"
  </rdfs:comment>
</rdf:Description>

<!-- ***** Component: Software ***** -->
<rdf:Description rdf:ID="AudioFormats">
  <rdf:type rdf:resource="http://www.w3.org/1999/02/22-rdf-syntax-ns#Property"/>
  <rdf:type rdf:resource="http://www.w3.org/1999/02/22-rdf-syntax-ns#Seq"/>
  <rdfs:domain rdf:resource="#Software"/>
  <rdfs:comment>
    Description:  Sorted list of audio formats, supported by the device.
                 Property value is a list of MIME types, where each item in the
                 list is a content type descriptor as specified by RFC 2045.
    Type:        Literal (Seq)
    Example:     "audio/mp4", "audio/mpa", "audio/mpeg"
  </rdfs:comment>
</rdf:Description>
```

```
<rdf:Description rdf:ID="VideoFormats">
  <rdf:type rdf:resource="http://www.w3.org/1999/02/22-rdf-syntax-ns#Property"/>
  <rdf:type rdf:resource="http://www.w3.org/1999/02/22-rdf-syntax-ns#Seq"/>
  <rdfs:domain rdf:resource="#Software"/>
  <rdfs:comment>
    Description:  Sorted list of video formats supported by the device.
                 Property value is a list of MIME types, where each item in the
                 list is a content type descriptor as specified by RFC 2045.
    Type:        Literal (Seq)
    Examples:    "video/H263", "video/H264", "video/mp4", "video/mpeg"
  </rdfs:comment>
</rdf:Description>

<rdf:Description rdf:ID="OSName">
  <rdf:type rdf:resource="http://www.w3.org/1999/02/22-rdf-syntax-ns#Property"/>
  <rdfs:domain rdf:resource="#Software"/>
  <rdfs:comment>
    Description:  Name of the device's operating system.
    Type:        Literal
    Examples:    "Mac OS", "Windows Mobile"
  </rdfs:comment>
</rdf:Description>

<rdf:Description rdf:ID="OSVendor">
  <rdf:type rdf:resource="http://www.w3.org/1999/02/22-rdf-syntax-ns#Property"/>
  <rdfs:domain rdf:resource="#Software"/>
  <rdfs:comment>
    Description:  Vendor of the device's operating system.
    Type:        Literal
    Examples:    "Apple", "Microsoft"
  </rdfs:comment>
</rdf:Description>

<rdf:Description rdf:ID="OSVersion">
  <rdf:type rdf:resource="http://www.w3.org/1999/02/22-rdf-syntax-ns#Property"/>
  <rdfs:domain rdf:resource="#Software"/>
  <rdfs:comment>
    Description:  Version of the device's operating system.
    Type:        Literal
    Examples:    "6.0", "4.5"
  </rdfs:comment>
</rdf:Description>

<!-- ***** Component: User ***** -->
<rdf:Description rdf:ID="AudioVideoPreference">
  <rdf:type rdf:resource="http://www.w3.org/1999/02/22-rdf-syntax-ns#Property"/>
  <rdfs:domain rdf:resource="#User"/>
  <rdfs:comment>
    Description:  Specifies whether the user prefers audio or video data in case
                 of bad connections or conflicting parameters.
    Type:        Literal
    Examples:    "video", "audio", "none"
  </rdfs:comment>
</rdf:Description>

<rdf:Description rdf:ID="MinFrameRate">
  <rdf:type rdf:resource="http://www.w3.org/1999/02/22-rdf-syntax-ns#Property"/>
  <rdfs:domain rdf:resource="#User"/>
  <rdfs:comment>
    Description:  Specifies the minimum frame rate desired by the user.
                 Values are given in frames per second.
    Type:        Number
    Examples:    "15", "24"
  </rdfs:comment>
</rdf:Description>
```

```
<rdf:Description rdf:ID="MinAudioRate">
  <rdf:type rdf:resource="http://www.w3.org/1999/02/22-rdf-syntax-ns#Property"/>
  <rdfs:domain rdf:resource="#User"/>
  <rdfs:comment>
    Description:  This value represents the minimal audio data rate desired by
                  the user. The value is expressed in kbit/s.
    Type:         Number
    Examples:     "64", "128"
  </rdfs:comment>
</rdf:Description>


<rdf:Description rdf:ID="MinVideoRate">
  <rdf:type rdf:resource="http://www.w3.org/1999/02/22-rdf-syntax-ns#Property"/>
  <rdfs:domain rdf:resource="#User"/>
  <rdfs:comment>
    Description:  This value represents the minimal audio data rate desired by
                  the user. The value is expressed in kbit/s.
    Type:         Number
    Examples:     "64", "1024"
  </rdfs:comment>
</rdf:Description>


<rdf:Description rdf:ID="MinHeight">
  <rdf:type rdf:resource="http://www.w3.org/1999/02/22-rdf-syntax-ns#Property"/>
  <rdfs:domain rdf:resource="#User"/>
  <rdfs:comment>
    Description:  The height of the desired content in pixels.
    Type:         Number
    Examples:     "160", "640"
  </rdfs:comment>
</rdf:Description>


<rdf:Description rdf:ID="MinWidth">
  <rdf:type rdf:resource="http://www.w3.org/1999/02/22-rdf-syntax-ns#Property"/>
  <rdfs:domain rdf:resource="#User"/>
  <rdfs:comment>
    Description:  The width of the desired content in pixels.
    Type:         Number
    Examples:     "160", "640"
  </rdfs:comment>
</rdf:Description>


<!-- ***** Component: Priority ***** -->
<rdf:Description rdf:ID="Priorities">
  <rdf:type rdf:resource="http://www.w3.org/1999/02/22-rdf-syntax-ns#Property"/>
  <rdf:type rdf:resource="http://www.w3.org/1999/02/22-rdf-syntax-ns#Bag"/>
  <rdfs:domain rdf:resource="#Priority"/>
  <rdfs:comment>
    Description:  Specifies the priorities selected by the user for attributes
                  given in the other components, so that conflicts can be solved
                  according to the user's preferences.
                  Values may range from 0 (unimportant) to 100 (very important).
                  Each attribut should get a unique priority.
    Type:         Literal (Bag)
    Examples:     "ScreenSize=100", "MinVideoRate=75", "MinAudioRate=50"
  </rdfs:comment>
</rdf:Description>

</rdf:RDF>
```

A.2 RTSP Messages for Gateway Cooperation

The proposed cooperative caching scheme which is presented in section 3.3.5 uses several different messages to exchange information between cooperating gateways. As the gateways already use RTSP for signaling purposes, we implemented the cooperation messages embedded in RTSP messages. The design of RTSP allows future extension of the protocol by defining several optional messages. Two of these optional messages are the SET_PARAMETER and GET_PARAMETER messages. The former message should be used to set a certain parameter at the communication partner receiving such a message, whereas the latter message may be used to request a parameter from a communication partner.

For the proposed gateway cooperation we implemented the *neighbor* and *cache* messages by using the SET_PARAMETER message whereas the *peer* and *ping* messages are implemented by using the GET_PARAMETER message. In the following paragraphs we give some examples of all messages used for the proposed gateway cooperation mechanism.

Neighbor Message

A *neighbor* message is used for registering the sender of this message as a neighbor at the receiving gateway. The receiving gateway stores the IP-address and RTSP-port given in the body of this message into its neighbor list and sends any changes to its cached objects to this address.

Request:

```
SET_PARAMETER * RTSP/1.0
CSeq: 1
Content-Type: text/parameters
Content-Length: 26

neighbor: 127.0.0.1:1111
```

Response:

```
RTSP/1.0 200 OK
CSeq: 1
```

Cache Message

A *cache* message is used to inform the receiver of this message about any changes to cached objects at the sending gateway. The body of this message contains the IP-address and RTSP-port of the sender as well as information about cached objects.

Request:

```
SET_PARAMETER * RTSP/1.0
CSeq: 1
Content-Type: text/parameters
Content-Length: 101


cache_location: 134.169.35.201:1111
cached_object: gagel.mp4;0-360
cached_object: puh.mp4;0-135
```

Response:

```
RTSP/1.0 200 OK
CSeq: 1
```

Peer Message

A *peer* message can be used to request all registered peers from the receiver of this message. The body of the GET_PARAMETER message simply contains the word "peer". The receiver of this message sends a response that contains a list of IP-addresses and RTSP-ports of gateways at which the receiver is registered as a neighbor.

Request:

```
GET_PARAMETER * RTSP/1.0
CSeq: 1
Content-Type: text/parameters
Content-Length: 6


peer
```

Response:

```
RTSP/1.0 200 OK
CSeq: 1
Content-Type: text/parameters
Content-Length: 81


peer: 134.169.35.201:1111
peer: 134.169.35.202:2222
peer: 134.169.35.203:3333
```

Ping Message

A *ping* message can be used to check the existence of a remote gateway. This message may contain a timestamp that the receiver needs to copy into the response message. By the use of this timestamp the sender of a *ping* message may evaluate the network and processing delay for the receiving gateway. Further evaluation parameters such as the current processing load or available cache capacity could also be included in the response.

Request:

```
GET_PARAMETER * RTSP/1.0
CSeq: 1
Content-Type: text/parameters
Content-Length: 18


ping: 12345:6789
```

Response:

```
RTSP/1.0 200 OK
CSeq: 1
Content-Type: text/parameters
Content-Length: 18


ping: 12345:6789
```

Appendix B

Measurement Details

B.1 Visual Quality Measurement for Varying Spatial Resolutions

For evaluating the visual quality of some test sequences encoded at different spatial resolutions, we used the following tools: All video streams were encoded by using the MEncoder from the MPlayer project with the MPEG-4 codec from the FFMpeg project. For evaluating the visual quality we used the MPlayer to decode and scale the video frames to the original resolution. With these decoded and upscaled frames we were able to compute the PSNR values for each single frame. For all scaling processes involved during the evaluation we used the algorithm implemented in the MPlayer which is also used by the MEncoder. Therefore, the results could not be influenced by different scaling algorithms.

The following graphs show the results for all test sequences that were not already shown in section 4.1.2.

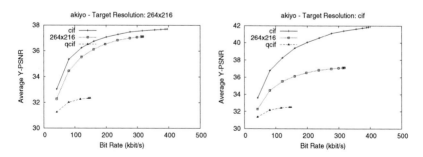

Figure B.1: Video quality at different spatial resolutions - akiyo sequence

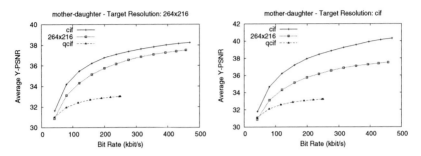

Figure B.2: Video quality at different spatial resolutions - mother-daughter sequence

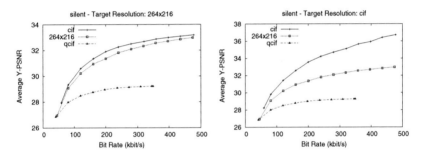

Figure B.3: Video quality at different spatial resolutions - silent sequence

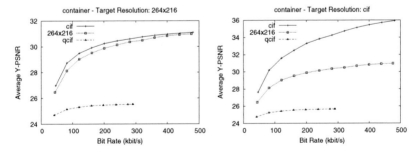

Figure B.4: Video quality at different spatial resolutions - container sequence

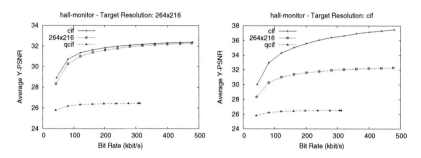

Figure B.5: Video quality at different spatial resolutions - hall-monitor sequence

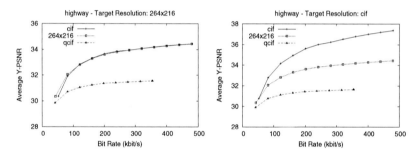

Figure B.6: Video quality at different spatial resolutions - highway sequence

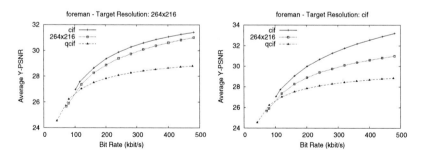

Figure B.7: Video quality at different spatial resolutions - foreman sequence

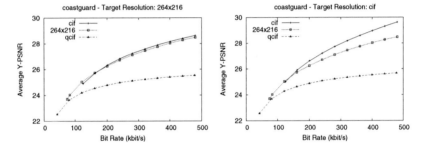

Figure B.8: Video quality at different spatial resolutions - coastguard sequence

B.2 Produced Quality of the Multidimensional MPEG-4 Transcoder

This section contains the graphs showing the quality of all test sequences produced by our multidimensional MPEG-4 transcoder implementation that were not already presented in section 4.2.6. For each test sequence we show the graphs for four differently adapted versions:

1. one version adapted solely in the detail dimension, denoted with "CIF 25 fps",

2. one version adapted in the temporal and detail dimension, denoted with "CIF 12.5 fps",

3. one version adapted in the spatial and detail dimension, denoted with "QCIF 25 fps",

4. one version adapted in all three dimensions, denoted with "QCIF 12.5 fps".

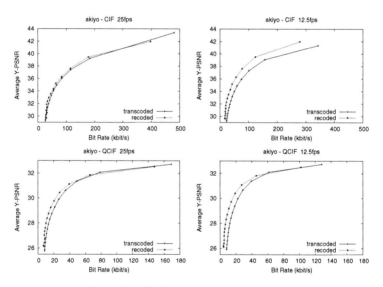

Figure B.9: Produced quality akiyo sequence

133

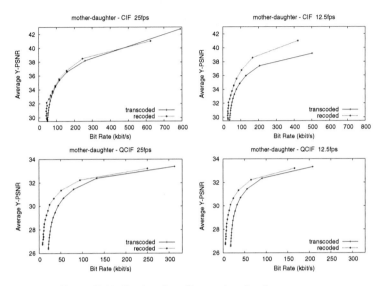

Figure B.10: Produced quality mother-daughter sequence

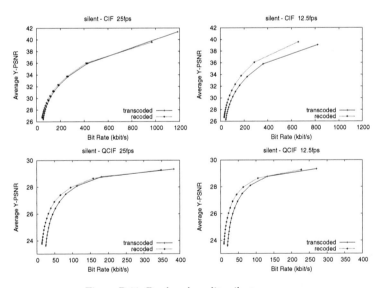

Figure B.11: Produced quality silent sequence

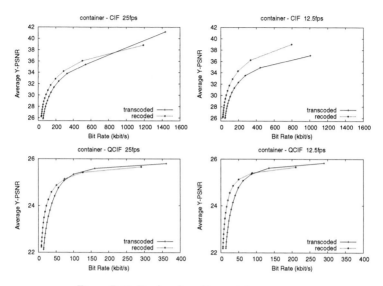

Figure B.12: Produced quality container sequence

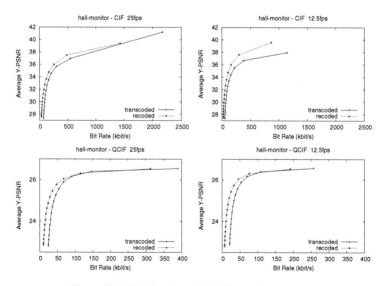

Figure B.13: Produced quality hall-monitor sequence

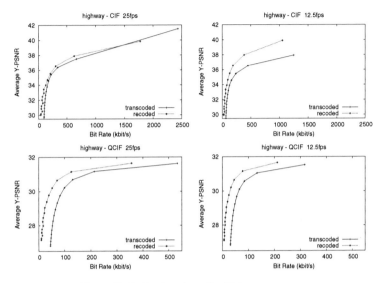

Figure B.14: Produced quality highway sequence

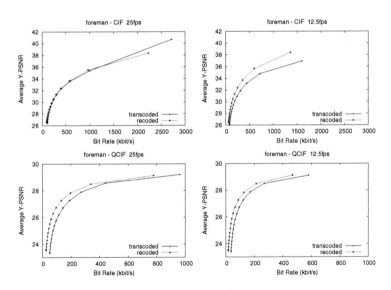

Figure B.15: Produced quality foreman sequence

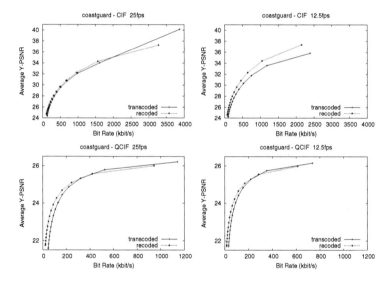

Figure B.16: Produced quality coastguard sequence

Bibliography

[1] ISO/IEC, "Coding of audio-visual objects – Part 2: Visual," ISO/IEC 14496-2 (MPEG-4 Video), Version 1: Apr. 1999, Version 2: Feb. 2000, Version 3: May 2004.

[2] *ANSI/IEEE Std 802.11-1999: Part 11: Wireless LAN Medium Access Control (MAC) and Physical Layer (PHY) Specifications*, Aug. 1999.

[3] J. Schiller, *Mobile Communications*, 2nd edition, Addison-Wesley, Aug. 2003.

[4] V. Kahmann, J. Brandt, and L. Wolf, "Flexible Media Reflection for Collaborative Streaming Scenarios," in *Proceedings of the IEEE Tenth International Workshop on Web Content Caching and Distribution*, Sophia Antipolis, France, Sept. 2005, pp. 71–76.

[5] J. Brandt, V. Kahmann, and L. Wolf, "A flexible reflector for media streams," in *KIVS, Kurzbeiträge und Workshop*, Mar. 2005, vol. PI-61 of *Lecture Notes in Informatics*, pp. 41–48.

[6] J. Brandt and L. Wolf, "A Gateway Architecture for Mobile Multimedia Streaming," in *European Symposium on Mobile Media Delivery (EuMob06)*, Alghero, Italy, Sept. 2006.

[7] J. Brandt and L. Wolf, "Multidimensional Transcoding for Adaptive Video Streaming," in *Proceedings of the 17th International Workshop on Network and Operating Systems Support for Digital Audio and Video (NOSSDAV'07)*, Urbana-Champaign, IL, USA, June 2007, pp. 57–62.

[8] J. Brandt and L. Wolf, "Adaptive Video Streaming for Mobile Clients," in *Proceedings of the 18th International workshop on Network and Operating Systems Support for Digital Audio and Video (NOSSDAV'08)*, Braunschweig, Germany, May 2008, pp. 113–114.

[9] J. Brandt, J. Trotzky, and L. Wolf, "Fast frame-based scene change detection in the compressed domain for mpeg-4 video," in *Proceedings of the Second International Conference on Next Generation Mobile Applications, Services, and Technologies (NGMAST '08)*, Cardiff, Wales, GB, Sept. 2008, pp. 514–520.

[10] ITU-T, "Video Codec for Audiovisual Services at p × 64 kbit/s," ITU-T Recommendation H.261, Version 1: Nov. 1990, Version 2: Mar. 1993.

[11] ISO/IEC, "Coding of Moving Pictures and Associated Audio for Digital Storage Media at up to About 1,5 Mbit/s – Part 2: Video," ISO/IEC 11172-2 (MPEG-1 Video), Mar. 1993.

[12] ISO/IEC, "Generic Coding of Moving Pictures and Associated Audio Information – Part 2: Video," ISAO/IEC 13818-2 (MPEG-2 Video), Nov. 1994.

[13] ITU-T, "Video Coding for Low Bit Rate Communication," ITU-T Recommendation H.263, Version 1: Nov. 1995, Version 2: Jan. 1998, Version 3: Nov. 2000.

[14] ISO/IEC and ITU-T, "Coding of audio-visual objects – Part 10: Advanced Video Coding," ISO/IEC 14496-10 (MPEG-4 AVC) and ITU-T Recommendation H.264, Version 1: May 2003, Version 2: May 2004, Version 3: Mar. 2005, Version 4: Sept. 2005, Version 5 and 6: June 2006, Version 7: Apr. 2007, Version 8: July 2007.

[15] N. Ahmed, T. Natarajan, and K. Rao, "Discrete Cosine Transfom," *IEEE Transactions on Computers*, vol. C-23, no. 1, pp. 90–93, Jan. 1974.

[16] E. Feig and S. Winograd, "Fast algorithms for the discrete cosine transform," *Signal Processing, IEEE Transactions on*, vol. 40, no. 9, pp. 2174–2193, Sept. 1992.

[17] D. Huffman, "A method for the construction of minimum-redundancy codes," *Proceedings of the IRE*, vol. 40, no. 9, pp. 1098–1101, Sept. 1952.

[18] H. Schulzrinne, A. Rao, and R. Lanphier, "Real Time Streaming Protocol (RTSP)," RFC 2326, Internet Engineering Task Force (IETF), Apr. 1998.

[19] H. Schulzrinne, S. Casner, R. Frederick, and V. Jacobson, "RTP: A Transport Protocol for Real-Time Applications," RFC 3550, Internet Engineering Task Force (IETF), July 2003.

[20] J. Postel, "User Datagram Protocol," RFC 768, Aug. 1980.

[21] M. Handley, V. Jacobson, and C. Perkins, "SDP: Session Description Protocol," RFC 4566, Internet Engineering Task Force (IETF), July 2006.

[22] J. van der Meer, D. Mackie, V. Swaminathan, D. Singer, and P. Gentric, "RTP Payload Format for Transport of MPEG-4 Elementary Streams," RFC 3640, Internet Engineering Task Force (IETF), Nov. 2003.

[23] A. Sinha, G. Agarwal, and A. Anbu, "Region-of-interest based compressed domain video transcoding scheme," in *Proceedings of the IEEE International Conference on Acoustics, Speech, and Signal Processing, (ICASSP '04)*, Montreal, Canada, May 2004.

[24] H. Schwarz, D. Marpe, and T. Wiegand, "Overview of the Scalable Video Coding Extension of the H.264/AVC Standard," *IEEE Transactions on Circuits and Systems for Video Technology*, vol. 17, no. 9, pp. 1103–1120, Sept. 2007.

[25] M. Wien, H. Schwarz, and T. Oelbaum, "Performance Analysis of SVC," *IEEE Transactions on Circuits and Systems for Video Technology*, vol. 17, no. 9, pp. 1194–1203, Sept. 2007.

[26] R. Rejaie and J. Kangasharju, "Mocha: A quality adaptive multimedia proxy cache for internet streaming," in *Proceedings of the 11th International Workshop on Network and Operating Systems Support for Digital Audio and Video (NOSSDAV '01)*, Port Jefferson, NY, USA, June 2001, pp. 3–10.

[27] Q. Zhang, Z. Xiang, W. Zhu, and L. Gao, "Cost-based cache replacement and server selection for multimedia proxy across wireless Internet," *IEEE Transactions on Multimedia*, vol. 6, no. 4, pp. 587 – 598, Aug. 2004.

[28] I. Kofler, M. Prangl, R. Kuschnig, and H. Hellwagner, "An H.264/SVC-based adaptation proxy on a WiFi router," in *Proceedings of the 18th International Workshop on Network and Operating Systems Support for Digital Audio and Video (NOSSDAV '08)*, Braunschweig, Germany, May 2008, pp. 63–68.

[29] J. Liu, B. Li, and Y.-Q. Zhang, "Adaptive video multicast over the Internet," *IEEE Multimedia*, vol. 10, no. 1, pp. 22 – 33, Jan. 2003.

[30] S. R. McCanne, V. Jacobson, and M. Vetterli, "Receiver-driven layered multicast," in *Conference proceedings on Applications, Technologies, Architectures, and Protocols for Computer Communications*, Palo Alto, NY, USA, Aug. 1996, pp. 117–130.

[31] B. Vickers, C. Albuquerque, and T. Suda, "Source-adaptive multi-layered multicast algorithms for real-time video distribution," *IEEE/ACM Transactions on Networking*, vol. 8, no. 6, pp. 720–733, Dec. 2000.

[32] T. Shanableh and M. Ghanabari, "Multilayer transcoding with format portability for multicasting of single-layered video," *IEEE Transactions on Multimedia*, vol. 7, no. 1, pp. 1 – 15, Feb. 2005.

[33] S. Liu and C.-C. Kuo, "Joint temporal-spatial rate control for adaptive video transcoding," in *Proceedings of the International Conference on Multimedia and Expo (ICME'03)*, Baltimore, MD, USA, July 2003, vol. 2, pp. 225–228.

[34] J. Youn, M.-T. Sun, and J. Xin, "Video transcoder architectures for bit rate scaling of H.263 bit streams," in *Proceedings of the seventh ACM international conference on Multimedia (ACM MULTIMEDIA '99)*, Orlando, FL, USA, Nov. 1999, pp. 243–250.

[35] A. Vetro, C. Christopoulos, and H. Sun, "Video transcoding architectures and techniques: an overview," *IEEE Signal Processing Magazine*, vol. 20, no. 2, pp. 18–29, Mar. 2003.

[36] T. C. Huifang Sun, Xeumin Chen, *Digital Video Transcoding for Transmission and Storage*, CRC Press, 2005.

[37] S.-F. Chang and D. G. Messerschmitt, "Manipulation and Compositing of MC-DCT Compressed Video," *IEEE Journal on Selected Areas in Communications*, vol. 13, no. 1, pp. 1–11, Jan. 1995.

[38] N. Merhav and V. Bhaskaran, "Fast algorithms for DCT-domain image downsampling and for inverse motion compensation," *IEEE Transactions on Circuits and Systems for Video Technology*, vol. 7, no. 3, pp. 468–476, June 1997.

[39] J. Song and B.-L. Yeo, "A fast algorithm for DCT-domain inverse motion compensation based on shared information in a macroblock," *IEEE Transactions on Circuits and Systems for Video Technology*, vol. 10, no. 5, pp. 767–775, Aug. 2000.

[40] S. Liu and A. C. Bovik, "A Fast and Memory Efficient Video Transcoder for Low Bit Rate Wireless Communications," in *IEEE International Conference on Acoustics, Speech, and Signal Processing, 2002. Proceedings. (ICASSP '02)*, Orlando, FL, USA, May 2002, vol. 2, pp. 1969–1972.

[41] V. Patil and R. Kumar, "A Fast Inverse Motion Compensation Algorithm for DCT-Domain Video Transcoder," *IEEE Transactions on Circuits and Systems for Video Technology*, vol. 18, no. 3, pp. 394–399, March 2008.

[42] P. A. Assuncao and M. Ghanbari, "A Frequency-Domain Video Transcoder for Dynamic Bit-Rate Reduction of MPEG-2 Bit Streams," *IEEE Transactions on Circuits and Systems for Video Technology*, vol. 8, no. 8, pp. 953–967, Dec. 1998.

[43] J.-N. Hwang, T.-D. Wu, and C.-W. Lin, "Dynamic frame skipping in video transcoding," in *Proceedings of the IEEE Second Workshop on Multimedia Signal Processing*, Redondo Beach, CA, USA, Dec. 1998, pp. 616–621.

[44] J. Youn, M.-T. Sun, and C.-W. Lin, "Motion vector refinement for high performance transcoding," *IEEE Transactions on Multimedia*, vol. 1, no. 1, pp. 30–40, Mar. 1999.

[45] M.-J. Chen, M.-C. Chu, and C.-W. Pan, "Efficient Motion-Estimation Algorithm for Reduced Frame-Rate Video Transcoder," *IEEE Transactions on Circuits and Systems for Video Technology*, vol. 12, no. 4, pp. 269–275, Apr. 2002.

[46] K.-T. Fung, Y.-L. Chan, and W.-C. Siu, "Dynamic frame-skipping for high-performance transcoding," in *Proceedings of the IEEE International Conference on Image Processing*, Thessaloniki, Greece, Oct. 2001, vol. 1, pp. 425–428.

[47] K.-T. Fung, Y.-L. Chan, and W.-C. Siu, "New Architecture for Dynamic Frame-Skipping Transcoder," *IEEE Transactions on Image Processing*, vol. 11, no. 8, pp. 886–900, Aug. 2002.

[48] K.-T. Fung and W.-C. Siu, "DCT-based video frame-skipping transcoder," in *Proceedings of the IEEE International Symposium on Circuits and Systems (IS-CAS '03)*, Bangkok, Thailand, May 2003, vol. 2, pp. 656–659.

[49] T. Shanableh and M. Ghanbari, "Heterogeneous video transcoding to lower spatio-temporal resolutions and different encoding formats," *IEEE Transactions on Multimedia*, vol. 2, no. 2, pp. 101–110, June 2000.

[50] P. Yin, A. Vetro, H. Sun, and B. Liu, "Drift Compensation for Reduced Resolution Transcoding," *IEEE Transactions on Circuits and Systems for Video Technology*, vol. 12, no. 11, pp. 1009–1020, Nov. 2002.

[51] X. Yu, E. hui Yang, and H. Wang, "Down-Sampling Design in DCT Domain With Arbitrary Ratio for Image/Video Transcoding," *IEEE Transactions on Image Processing*, vol. 18, no. 1, pp. 75–89, Jan. 2009.

[52] N. Roma and L. Sousa, "Efficient hybrid DCT-domain algorithm for video spatial downscaling," *EURASIP Journal on Advances in Signal Processing*, vol. 2007, no. 2, pp. 30–30, June 2007.

[53] R. Dugad and N. Ahuja, "A Fast Scheme for Image Size Change in the Compressed Domain," *IEEE Transactions on Circuits and Systems for Video Technology*, vol. 11, no. 4, pp. 461–474, Apr. 2001.

[54] C. Salazar-Lazaro and T. D. Tran, "On resizing images in the dct domain," in *in Proceedings of the IEEE International Conference on Image Processing, (ICIP '04)*, Singapore, Oct. 2004, vol. 4, pp. 2797–2800.

[55] J. Mukherjee and S. Mitra, "Arbitrary resizing of images in DCT space," *IEE Proceedings - Vision, Image and Signal Processing*, vol. 152, no. 2, pp. 155–164, Apr. 2005.

[56] Y.-R. Lee and C.-W. Lin, "Visual Quality Enhancement in DCT-Domain Spatial Downscaling Transcoding Using Generalized DCT Decimation," *IEEE Transactions on Circuits and Systems for Video Technology*, vol. 17, no. 8, pp. 1079–1084, Aug. 2007.

[57] Y.-R. Lee, C.-W. Lin, and C.-C. Kao, "A DCT-Domain Video Transcoder for Spatial Resolution Downconversion," *Lecture Notes in Computer Science*, , no. 2314, pp. 207–218, Mar. 2002.

[58] B. Shen and S. Roy, "A Very Fast Video Spatial Resolution Reduction Transcoder," in *IEEE International Conference on Acoustics, Speech and Signal Processing (ICASSP '02)*, Orlando, FL, USA, May 2002, vol. 2, pp. 1989–1992.

[59] A. Vetro and H. Sun, "Media conversion to support mobile users," in *IEEE Canadian Conference on Electronic and Computer Engineering*, Toronto, Canada, May 2001, vol. 1, pp. 607–612.

[60] S. Wee, J. Apostolopoulos, T. Wai-tian, and S. Roy, "Research and design of a mobile streaming media content delivery network," in *Proceedings of the International Conference on Multimedia and Expo (ICME'03)*, Baltimore, MD, USA, July 2003, vol. 1, pp. 5–8.

[61] K. Hashimoto and Y. Shibata, "Extended video stream by media transcoding functions," in *Proceedings of the 24th International Conference on Distributed Computing Systems Workshops*, Tokyo, Japan, Mar. 2004, pp. 16 – 21.

[62] E. Amir, S. McCanne, and H. Zhang, "An Application Level Video Gateway," in *Proceedings of the Third ACM International Conference on Multimedia '95*, San Francisco, CA, USA, Nov. 1995, pp. 255–265.

[63] C.-H. Chi and Y. Cao, "Progressive proxy-based multimedia transcoding system with maximum data reuse," in *Proceedings of the 10th ACM International Conference on Multimedia 2002*, Juan les Pins, France, Dec. 2002, pp. 425–426.

[64] J. Guo, F. Chen, L. Bhuyan, and R. Kumar, "A cluster-based active router architecture supporting video/audio stream transcoding service," in *Proceedings of the 17th International Parallel and Distributed Processing Symposium (IPDPS'03)*, Nice, France, Apr. 2003, pp. 44–51.

[65] Z. Lei and N. D. Georganas, "Video transcoding gateway for wireless video access," in *IEEE Canadian Conference on Electronic and Computer Engineering*, Montreal, Canada, May 2003, vol. 3, pp. 1775–1778.

[66] P. Schojer, L. Böszörmenyi, H. Hellwagner, B. Penz, and S. Podlipnig, "Architecture of a quality based intelligent proxy (QBIX) for MPEG-4 videos," in

Proceedings of the twelfth international conference on World Wide Web (WWW '03), Budapest, Hungary, May 2003, pp. 394–402.

[67] S. Roy, M. Covell, J. A. S. Wee, and T. Yoshimura, "A system architecture for managing mobile streaming media services," in *Proceedings of the 23rd International Conference on Distributed Computing Systems Workshops*, Providence, RI, USA, May 2003, pp. 408–413.

[68] S. Roy, J. Ankcorn, and S. Wee, "Architecture of a modular streaming media server for content delivery networks," in *Proceedings of the International Conference on Multimedia and Expo (ICME'03)*, Baltimore, MD, USA, July 2003, vol. 3, pp. 569–572.

[69] M. Hemy, U. Hengartner, P. Steenkiste, and T. Gross, "MPEG System Streams in Best-Effort Networks," in *Packet Video Workshop*, New York, USA, Apr. 1999.

[70] Z. M. Mao, H.-S. W. So, and B. Kang, "Network support for mobile multimedia using a self-adaptive distributed proxy," in *Proceedings of the 11th International Workshop on Network and Operating Systems Support for Digital Audio and Video (NOSSDAV '01)*, Port Jefferson, NY, USA, June 2001, pp. 107–116.

[71] K. Hashimoto and Y. Shibata, "Design of a middleware system for flexible intercommunication environment," in *Proceedings of the 17th International Conference on Advanced Information Networking and Applications (AINA'03)*, Xi'an, China, Mar. 2003, pp. 59–64.

[72] K. Hashimoto and Y. Shibata, "Dynamic transcoding functions by extended media stream," in *Proceedings of the 18th International Conference on Advanced Information Networking and Applications (AINA 2004)*, Fukuoka, Japan, Mar. 2004, pp. 334 – 339.

[73] B. Duysburgh, T. Lambrecht, B. Dhoedt, and P. Demeester, "On the quality and performance of active networking based media transcoding in multicast sessions," in *Proceedings of the 7th International Conference on Telecommunications*, June 2003, vol. 2, pp. 455–462.

[74] B. Duysburgh, T. Lambrecht, F. DeTurck, B. Dhoedt, and P. Demeester, "An Active Networking Based Service for Media Transcoding in Multicast Sessions," *IEEE Transactions on Systems, Man and Cybernetics, Part C*, vol. 34, no. 1, pp. 19–31, Feb. 2004.

[75] S. Winkler and P. Mohandas, "The Evolution of Video Quality Measurement: From PSNR to Hybrid Metrics," *IEEE Transactions on Broadcasting*, vol. 54, no. 3, pp. 660–668, Sept. 2008.

[76] B. Girod, "What's wrong with mean-squared error?," *Digital images and human vision*, pp. 207–220, 1993.

[77] Q. Huynh-Thu and M. Ghanbari, "Scope of validity of PSNR in image/video quality assessment," *IET Electronics Letters*, vol. 44, no. 13, pp. 800–801, June 2008.

[78] J. Youn and M.-T. Sun, "Video Transcoding with H.263 Bit-Streams," *Journal of Visual Communication and Image Representation*, vol. 11, no. 4, pp. 385–403, Dec. 2000.

[79] R. G. Herrtwich and L. Wolf, "A system software structure for distributed multimedia systems," in *Proceedings of the 5th workshop on ACM SIGOPS European workshop*, Mont Saint-Michel, France, Sept. 1992, pp. 1–5.

[80] V. Kahmann, J. Brandt, and L. Wolf, "Collaborative Streaming in Heterogeneous and Dynamic Scenarios," *Communications of the ACM, Special Issue on Entertainment Networking*, vol. 49, no. 11, pp. 58–63, Nov. 2006.

[81] V. Kahmann, *Collaborative Media Streaming*, Ph.D. thesis, Technische Universität Braunschweig, Germany, July 2008.

[82] G. G. Richard, "Service Advertisement and Discovery: Enabling Universal Device Cooperation," *IEEE Internet Computing*, vol. 4, no. 5, pp. 18–26, Oct. 2000.

[83] M. Bechler, O. Storz, W. Franz, and L. Wolf, "Efficient Discovery of Internet Gateways in Future Vehicular Communication Systems," in *IEEE Semiannual Vehicular Technology Conference, Jeju, Korea*, Apr. 2003, vol. 2, pp. 965–969.

[84] E. Guttman, C. Perkins, J. Veizades, and M. Day, "Service Location Protocol, Version 2," RFC 2608, Internet Engineering Task Force (IETF), June 1999.

[85] G. Klyne, F. Reynolds, C. Woodrow, H. Ohto, J. Hjelm, M. H. Butler, and L. Tran, "Composite Capability/Preference Profiles (CC/PP): Structure and Vocabularies 1.0," W3C Recommendation, Jan. 2004, http://www.w3.org/TR/CCPP-struct-vocab/.

[86] F. Manola and E. Miller, "Resource Description Framework," W3C Recommendation, Feb. 2004, http://www.w3.org/TR/REC-rdf-syntax/.

[87] S. Roy, B. Shen, V. Sundaram, and R. Kumar, "Application level hand-off support for mobile media transcoding sessions," in *Proceedings of the 12th international workshop on Network and operating systems support for digital audio and video (NOSSDAV '02)*, Miami Beach, FL, USA, May 2002, pp. 95–104.

[88] S. Sen, J. Rexford, and D. F. Towsley, "Proxy Prefix Caching for Multimedia Streams," in *Proceedings of the Eighteenth Annual Joint Conference of the IEEE Computer and Communications Societies, INFOCOM '99*, New York, NY, USA, Mar. 1999, vol. 3, pp. 1310–1319.

[89] H. Fahmi, M. Latif, S. Sedigh-Ali, A. Ghafoor, P. Liu, and L. Hsu, "Proxy Servers for Scalable Interactive Video Support," *IEEE Computer*, vol. 34, no. 9, pp. 54–59, Sept. 2001.

[90] A. Dan and D. Sitaram, "A Generalized Interval Caching Policy for Mixed Interactive and Long Video Workloads," in *Proceedings of the SPIE Multimedia Computing and Networking Conference*, San Jose, CA, USA, Jan. 1996, pp. 344–351.

[91] R. Tewari, H. M. Vin, A. Dan, and D. Sitaram, "Resource-based Caching for Web Servers," in *SPIE/ACM Conference on Multimedia Computing and Networking, MMCN '98*, San Jose, CA, Jan. 1998.

[92] K.-L. Wu, P. S. Yu, and J. L. Wolf, "Segment-based proxy caching of multimedia streams," in *Proceedings of the 10th international conference on World Wide Web (WWW '01)*, May 2001, pp. 36–44.

[93] S. Chen, B. Shen, S. Wee, and X. Zhang, "Adaptive and lazy segmentation based proxy caching for streaming media delivery," in *Proceedings of the 13th International Workshop on Network and Operating Systems Support for Digital Audio and Video (NOSSDAV '03)*, Monterey, CA, USA, June 2003, pp. 22–31.

[94] S. Chen, B. Shen, S. Wee, and X. Zhang, "Designs of high quality streaming proxy systems," in *Twenty-third AnnualJoint Conference of the IEEE Computer and Communications Societies (INFOCOM '04)*, Hong Kong, China, Mar. 2004, vol. 3, pp. 1512–1521.

[95] S. Park, Y. Lee, and H. Shin, "Quality-adaptive requantization for low-energy MPEG-4 video decoding in mobile devices," *IEEE Transactions on Consumer Electronics*, vol. 51, no. 3, pp. 999–1005, Aug. 2005.

[96] M. Li, M. Claypool, R. Kinicki, and J. Nichols, "Characteristics of streaming media stored on the Web," *ACM Transactions on Internet Technology (TOIT)*, vol. 5, no. 4, pp. 601–626, Nov. 2005.

[97] J. D. McCarthy, M. A. Sasse, and D. Miras, "Sharp or smooth?: comparing the effects of quantization vs. frame rate for streamed video," in *Proceedings of the SIGCHI conference on Human factors in computing systems (CHI '04)*, Vienna, Austria, Apr. 2004, pp. 535–542.

[98] A. Eichhorn and P. Ni, "Pick your Layers wisely - A Quality Assessment of H.264 Scalable Video Coding for Mobile Devices," in *IEEE International Conference on Communications, ICC '09*, Dresden, Germany, June 2009.

[99] E. Gamma, R. Helm, R. Johnson, and J. Vlissides, *Design Patterns: Elements of Reusable Object-Oriented Software*, Addison-Wesley, 1995.

[100] J. S. Boreczky and L. A. Rowe, "Comparison of video shot boundary detection techniques," in *Storage and Retrieval for Image and Video Databases (SPIE)*, San Diego/La Jolla, CA, USA, Jan. 1996, vol. 2420, pp. 170–179.

[101] J. Bescos, "Real-time shot change detection over online MPEG-2 video," *IEEE Transactions on Circuits and Systems for Video Technology*, vol. 14, no. 4, pp. 475–484, Apr. 2004.

[102] Z. Cernekova, C. Nikou, and I. Pitas, "Shot detection in video sequences using entropy-based metrics," in *Proceedings of the International Conference on Image Processing*, Rochester, NY, USA, Sept. 2002, vol. 3, pp. 421–424.

[103] R. Fablet and P. Bouthemy, "Motion Recognition Using Nonparametric Image Motion Models Estimated from Temporal and Multiscale Co-Ocurrence Statistics," *IEEE Transactions on Pattern Analysis and Machine Intelligence*, vol. 25, no. 12, pp. 1619–1624, Dec. 2003.

[104] J. M. Gauch, S. Gauch, S. Bouix, and X. Zhu, "Real Time Video Scene Detection and Classification," *Information Processing and Management*, vol. 35, no. 3, pp. 381–400, May 1999.

[105] J. Han, D. Farin, P. H. de With, and W. Lao, "Automatic Tracking Method for Sports Video Analysis," in *Int. Symposium on Information Theory in the Benelux*, Brussels, Belgium, May 2005, pp. 309–316.

[106] R. Joyce and B. Liu, "Temporal segmentation of video using frame and histogram space," *IEEE Transactions on Multimedia*, vol. 8, no. 1, pp. 130–140, Feb. 2006.

[107] D. Lelescu and D. Schonfeld, "Statistical sequential analysis for real-time video scene change detection on compressed multimedia bitstream," *IEEE Transactions on Multimedia*, vol. 5, no. 1, pp. 106–117, Mar. 2003.

[108] X. Qian, G. Liu, and R. Su, "Effective Fades and Flashlight Detection Based on Accumulating Histogram Difference," *IEEE Transactions on Circuits and Systems for Video Technology*, vol. 16, no. 10, pp. 1245–1258, Oct. 2006.

[109] K. Shen and J. Delp, "A fast algorithm for video parsing using MPEG compressed sequences," in *Proceedings of the International Conference on Image Processing*, Washington D.C., USA, Oct. 1995, vol. 2, pp. 2252–2255.

[110] F. Arman, A. Hsu, and M. Chiu, "Image processing on compressed data for large video databases," in *Proceedings of the First ACM International Conference on Multimedia '93*, Anaheim, CA, USA, Aug. 1993, pp. 267–272.

[111] J. Meng, Y. Juan, and S. Chang, "Scene change detection in a MPEG compressed video sequence," in *Storage and Retrieval for Image and Video Databases (SPIE)*, San Diego/La Jolla, CA, USA, Jan. 1995, vol. 2420, pp. 14–25.

[112] R. Jin, Y. Qi, and A. Hauptmann, "A Probabilistic Model for Camera Zoom Detection," *Proceedings of the 16th International Conference on Pattern Recognition (ICPR '02)*, vol. 3, pp. 859–862, Aug. 2002.

[113] I. Sethi and N. Patel, "A statistical approach to scene change detection," in *Storage and Retrieval for Image and Video Databases (SPIE)*, San Diego/La Jolla, CA, USA, Jan. 1995, vol. 2420, pp. 329–338.

[114] S.-C. Pei and Y.-Z. Chou, "Effective wipe detection in MPEG compressed video using macro block type information," *IEEE Transactions on Multimedia*, vol. 4, no. 3, pp. 309–319, Sept. 2002.

[115] P. Bouthemy, M. Gelgon, and F. Ganansia, "A unified approach to shot change detection and camera motion characterization," *IEEE Transactions on Circuits and Systems for Video Technology*, vol. 9, no. 7, pp. 1030–1044, Oct. 1999.

[116] C. Dorai and V. Kobla, "Generating Motion Descriptors from MPEG-2 Compressed HDTV Video for Content-Based Annotation and Retrieval," in *IEEE Third Workshop on Multimedia Signal Processing (MMSP)*, Florence, Italy, Sept. 1999, pp. 673–678.

[117] M. S. Toller, P. H. Lewis, and M. S. Nixon, "Video Segmentation using Combined Cues," in *Storage and Retrieval for Image and Video Databases (SPIE)*, San Jose, CA, USA, Dec. 1998, pp. 414–425.

[118] Anthony Vetro, "Transcoding, Scalable Coding, and Standardized Metadata," *Visual Content Processing and Representation*, vol. 2849, pp. 15–16, Sept. 2003.

[119] C.-S. Park, T.-S. Wang, J.-H. Kim, M.-C. Hwang, and S.-J. Ko, "Video transcoding to support playback at a random location for scalable video coding," *Consumer Electronics, IEEE Transactions on*, vol. 53, no. 1, pp. 227–234, Feb. 2007.

[120] J. De Cock, S. Notebaert, and R. Van de Walle, "Transcoding from h.264/avc to svc with cgs layers," in *IEEE International Conference on Image Processing, ICIP 2007*, San Antonio, Texas, USA, Sept. 2007, vol. 4, pp. 73–76.

[121] "User Agent Profiling Specification (UAProf)," Wireless Application Protocol Forum, Oct. 2001, http://www.openmobilealliance.org/tech/affiliates/wap/wap-248-uaprof-20011020-a.pdf.